What Matters at Work

Harry M. Webne-Behrman

What Matters at Work

ISBN: 9781653808533
Imprint: Independently published

Cover and book design by Nancy Mitchell

First printing edition 2020

harry.whatmatters@gmail.com
www.whatmattersatwork.ca

To Lisa, my Partner in all things that matter

Acknowledgments and Gratitude

A few years ago, I outlined a possible workshop that lay dormant for awhile. As we were beginning our significant transition after many years in Madison, Wisconsin to our new life in Ottawa, Ontario, my partner Lisa sent me an email: "I found this outline of a workshop you once sketched out... still relevant?" From that brief note came deeper reflections, conversations, and actions that created this project.

My gratitude to others runs deeper than most: While I like to consult and collaborate, much of my writing has historically been a more solitary exercise. This time, however, it has been a truly joyful collaboration with many others who have contributed their insights and suggestions along the way. To begin, I want to acknowledge early readers who served as sounding boards for the concept of What Matters at Work and the relevance of the ideas: Jim Barney, Libby Bestul, Sarah Carroll, Steve Davis, Jane Dymond, Darin Eich, Marian Farrior, and Kathleen Paris, all provided important feedback and encouragement for which I am most grateful. As the project proceeded and evolved, Julie Kovalaske became a crucial partner in piloting the lessons and readings as we co-facilitated the initial What Matters at Work Study Group: With about two dozen phenomenal participants, I learned a great deal about how the material was resonating (or not) with real learners applying these ideas to real situations. Thanks as well to Steve Catania for creating a virtual container in which such learning could be facilitated and documented.

You will notice sprinkled throughout the text various references to the University of Wisconsin–Madison. Over more than forty years, UW has provided a wonderful "sandbox" in which I have been able to experiment with ideas about education, group process, and the advancement of professional development. Some of the important partners in this work over the years include Sarah Carroll, Jay Ekleberry, Paul Evans, DeWayne Gallenberg, Joe Goss, Darin Harris, Roger Howard, Seema Kapani, Marian Laines, Larry Larmer, Katherine Loving, Blair Mathews, Christine Ray, Don Schutt, Hazel Symonette, and Alberto Vargas,. Indeed, the list could go on and on: While I believe the benefits have been mutual, I must express particular gratitude to this amazing university for taking the chance to pursue some very creative ideas that could well have failed. That includes this project, where the Office of Learning and Talent Development has provided important sponsorship for our pilot courses.

I knew that preparing a book for publication would require a different skill set, one that could take my black and white text and breathe visual life into it: Fortunately, I found a wonderful collaborator in my friend Nancy Mitchell, that rare colleague who both understands the essence of these ideas and possesses great artistic and aesthetic capacities that translate to virtual layout design. She has been a total wonder to work with, offering her insights with generosity and professionalism. Similarly, I had hoped I could turn to my good friend Jane Dymond for her editing eyes late in the process, and she generously offered her keen skills to the text; she caught things that would certainly have eluded me otherwise.

As always, I am grateful for the encouragement of my family and friends these past two years as I've plugged along. But beyond such statements, I am most deeply aware of the many ways my Partner in Life and Work, Lisa, continues to enrich my insights and deepen the quality of my work. She has offered valuable reactions and suggestions to the text and the entire scope of this project as it has evolved, and many of the exercises contained herein reflect our joint efforts through thirty years of practice together.

I hope you like what has emerged from all of these contributions. While others have certainly added value, any flaws that remain are learning points where I want to continue to improve as we move beyond this text into other teaching and learning associated with this project. Please let me know what works, what doesn't, where you want new ideas, etc. In that way, my circle of collaborators can broaden and the strength of the ideas and practices can continue to focus on *What Matters at Work*.

Harry M. Webne-Behrman
November 2019
Ottawa, Ontario, Canada

CONTENTS

Prepare for the Journey

Survey the Terrains of Organizational Culture

Explore Pathways and Practices

Sustain the Journey - Nourish Yourself and Others

Launch the Journey

Learn Together to Deepen Capacity

PROLOGUE: WHAT MATTERS TO ME

The Workplace is a critical, high stakes environment. We are expected to be available at all hours, across modes and platforms, all for some vague priorities of customer service. We spend much of our lives in the world of work, spending most of our waking hours contemplating how best to earn a living. While we may practically need to "punch the clock" each day, we rarely give one another permission, encouragement, and support to develop more intentional, well-considered ways of approaching such time with a deeper sense of purpose.

Fortunately, there is a quiet, powerful revolution occurring within the 21st century organization, and we can notice these forces, harvest their practices, and build upon their insights to focus on What Matters. ***That's where this Guide comes in: To reflect on What Matters at Work is to reflect upon what has been learned and to apply to the pragmatic realities of work life.***

These strategies and approaches are intended to be applied in highly practical ways, across a vast swath of organizational cultures. We need to notice the right things to act upon, so we use our resources and talents in cost-effective ways. We need to raise concerns when they are required, halting potential courses of action that can damage our organization and those we serve. And we need to be clear regarding what is actually useful, rather than engaging in ego-gratifying jousts with "shiny objects" that grab our attention. If you want to engage in leadership that makes a difference on the bottom line, you had better be focused on What Matters at Work.

My own Journey has brought me to this place: I've worked as an educator, mediator, consultant, and facilitator. I've headed several organizations and offices, most of which I’ve built from scratch. I’ve helped others nurture their organizations, especially at times of change, challenge, and conflict. I've learned a few things about how to build, sustain, and repair organizations, and I've noticed several approaches that seem to work.

I have more to say and do: I feel a strong urge to remain engaged with the world of work, to share insights and strategies I have found successful through the years. I want to continue to work with others to understand their challenges, and figure out together how to successfully navigate them. Thus, I’m motivated to write, teach, and continue to explore these things that have been at the heart of my own work life these past forty-plus years.

The ideas in this Guide have been collected, adapted, revised, and synthesized through decades of practice. They include many activities that I have used in my consulting and teaching, which I gladly share with you now. I am grateful to the numerous people whose wisdom is tapped here and encourage you to find their writings and explore them more fully (please read the Endnotes and Bibliography). It is through such exploration that you can best integrate the learning from What Matters at Work into your own work and life: Taking the time to do so is a powerful investment in your capacity to provide leadership that can transform your organization.

If these ideas help you start or continue conversations that result in deep personal reflection and actions that improve your own sense of purpose, you have my gratitude for joining me in such a profound experience.

HOW TO USE THIS BOOK

This curriculum is presented as a series of concepts, exercises, conversations, reflections, and applications. While framed for individuals, they are also intended for learners experiencing these exercises together as a learning community or work team. Each knowledge and insight in a linear and sequential manner. As such, please consider this curriculum as a Guide that you, as the one taking the Journey, have final say regarding how long you linger on certain points. You determine how you choose to delve more deeply with your colleagues, or how you integrate what has been learned into your organization and into your personal work experience.

This Guide contains dozens of activities and worksheets – please make copies to share with colleagues! Our intention is for you to learn with others, and while we would appreciate groups purchasing multiple copies of the book, the worksheets are meant to be copied to meet your needs.

Lessons

This book is organized as a series of thirty-three Lessons, each with a particular focus on What Matters. The sequence proceeds from more individualized, introspective reflections into concepts that explore the structures and practices of your organization and how you may align business activities with the things that are most important to address. While each Lesson is fairly brief, many offer opportunities to linger and reflect on the ideas being offered: To reflect on What Matters may mean examining assumptions and norms that have gone unquestioned.

Exercises

Exercises appear throughout the text. *Try them out!* Some are Solo, others involve Pairs, Groups, or even Multiple Groups.

Challenges

Challenges are special exercises appearing later in the book. These combine two or three processes and apply them to difficult situations. They take longer to complete, but are critical to our overall Journey. Give them a try and involve your colleagues in What Matters at Work!

Wanderings

Diversions are important. We enter worlds of wonder when we allow ourselves to diverge from the appointed path, often to make profound discoveries that change our lives. Scattered throughout this Guide are "Wandering" reflections intended to expand your range of possibilities, perhaps to offer new perspectives on old questions. Sometimes, we benefit far more in our overall learning by following the crooked path, the tangential inquiry, the creative spark that arouses our curiosity. Just remember to leave breadcrumbs, or share that you've 'checked out' for awhile, so you can find your way back and others won't worry when you can't be found at your desk.[1]

Scenarios

Scenarios represent common workplace conflicts or dilemmas. Small groups can use these situations to practice and improve skills in important areas.

Worksheets

These are all printed at the end of the book, for you to complete as you make your way through the Guide. They may be freely copied and shared with others.

Prepare for the Journey

LESSON 1: NOTICE WHAT MATTERS

"We shall not cease from exploration.
And the end of all of our exploring
Will be to arrive where we started
And know the place for the first time."
- T. S. Eliot, Little Gidding (1942)

How do we best engage in What Matters? It all starts with Intention, that clarity of purpose to notice those things that matter and then act in a way that is consistent with what is important. Intention is course-setting, the compass that helps us navigate our way through the challenges and complexities of our days, weeks, years, and lives. Intention connects us with the core motivators of life, to offer a great contribution in service to the universe, to leave the world better than we entered, to be loving and caring friends, partners, parents, and citizens.

Taking the time to set intentions sounds simple enough, yet we tend to jump into the work day with little such thought. Instead, we usually react and respond to those immediate urgencies that call out to us from our Inbox, To-Do List, and appointment calendars. We get caught in the weeds of trivial detail, and the next thing we know it is well through the day. So, instead of just jumping into the day, take a few moments to set your Intention for the day. This ritual needn't be complicated or time-consuming. It is a simple process of sitting still, breathing deeply, and noticing those things that matter to you on this day... how you wish to Be, rather than what you wish to Do. This mindful process is the first step.

Exercise: Setting Intention for the Day

WHO: Solo

WHY: To prepare oneself to focus on What Matters, so there is clarity in mind and body that helps us notice our Intentions and priorities.

HOW:

Step 1 - Be seated comfortably, whether in your home or at your office. Close your eyes and breathe deeply several times. In your own words (silently or aloud), welcome the day.

Step 2 - With each breath, notice an Intention that wants to emerge, such as to be patient, supportive, tolerant of others' ideas, a good listener today.

Step 3 - After a minute, restate those 2-3-4 Intentions that you will seek to fulfill on this day, reminded with each deep breath you notice throughout the day.

As I reflect on what I've just asked you to do, I realize how foreign this may be for you. Many of us simply put one step in front of the other, with little time to reflect upon where we are going or why we are going there: it is simply "the way things are" and the way they need to be. To set an Intention for the day is to pause that process, not to abandon it. It is critically important in order to be sure that we are actually heading in the right direction. As a practical matter, it keeps us from wasting our time, staying productive in the face of distractions or stressors. As a spiritual matter, it grounds us and fills our souls with the energy required to breathe, keep breathing, and be fully alive. So give it a try, notice how it feels, and then try it repeatedly each day for a week. I expect you will notice some things that I can't begin to convey on these pages.

Intention also helps us focus our attention on what matters most: As we take time during our day to breathe and remember our Intention, we can also do a quick self "check-in": "Am I focused on my Intention?" *"Does my* ***attention*** *match my Intention?"* This can help us stay on track and be more mindful of What Matters.

LESSON 2: TAKE HEALTHY STEPS

Our society tends to reward and reinforce "busy-ness". We somehow think ourselves inadequate if our reply to others asking, *"So, how are you doing?"* is anything less than, *"Wow...things are really busy for me these days!"* It's a badge of honor, a source of pride, and a core element of professional and personal identity to be flitting from place to place, multi-tasking, and then "playing hard" to the degree time allows it. Of course, we may simply continue to be swamped with chauffeuring kids, attending more meetings, or otherwise filling our proverbial plates: We are BUSY, and there seems to be little incentive to change.

In his thought-provoking book, *Essentialism* (2014), author Greg McKeown invites us to focus solely on those things that really matter. He offers several approaches that dovetail quite well with things we've noticed, summarized in three core practices:

- Do Less, But Better
- Be Committed to the Rigorous Pursuit of Less
- Focus on the Essential

The practice that we wish to reinforce at this point is to Take Healthy Steps. This relates to focusing on the Essential, but it also means noticing that as we go from place to place, we take our Intention with us and incorporate a sense of Beauty and Appreciation, as well.

I make an effort to take at least 10,000 steps each day, as this is one way I bring my intention to stay fit and upright into my routine. But I do more than merely walk from place to place: I try to bring "spring" in my step, noticing my energy level and state of being, perhaps singing to myself for part of the journey. I try to notice the world around me, the sun and trees and people, and appreciate that by walking about I am able to notice very different things than when I drive.

I have also noticed over the years that, as I walk the areas where I work or live, I meet people I know; this is a great opportunity to connect regarding a project or an idea, or simply to be with friends and colleagues. This awareness has resulted in generally trying to leave an extra few minutes for that walk, so I don't resent meeting people I want to see. If no such encounter occurs, it allows me the time to notice my environment a bit more completely and refocus my attention on the meeting about to occur before I enter the space where it will happen. As we discuss elsewhere, ***relationships are the fundamental building blocks of Community;*** such encounters are actually "work" that is productive, if kept in proper proportion to the other purposes at hand.

My partner, Lisa, is a voracious walker and has been for many years. Every year for her birthday, she selects a hike and thinks through some of the key milestones along the route. She dedicates this anniversary of her birth as a day of reflection and renewal, both in intellectual terms and in physical terms. Together, we also chart out regular hikes, and consider such events to be excellent ways to both connect together and to have conversations about dilemmas in our work and our family. All along the way, we try to stride in a manner consistent with our broader intentions.

As a result, I often have time for **Connection** (when walking with Lisa), **Reflection** (alone), and **Synthesis** (to/from meetings). Each aspect matters, and it dawns on me that we don't often allow such a routine to offer us these important ingredients. My 'quality of life' tends to be better when all three ingredients feed one another on a given day. If I Connect with people, especially those important in my life, I tend to be stimulated, energized, and purposeful. Whether I am in Working or Relational mode, I get nourished by interesting conversation about worthy topics. It takes time, and it doesn't happen in the rushed formalities of e-mail encounters.

Lastly, Synthesis allows the opportunity to make sense of all we experience, sort out the nuggets of life lessons, and determine what is worth acting upon and how best to do so. Synthesis helps us sort the "Urgency/Importance" matrix and find the meaningful currents in our work - otherwise, we are likely to respond without taking proper stock of the best pathways before us. As we will discuss later around Wellness and Well-Being, the workplace needs to support such behaviors as an integral element of an organization that focuses on What Matters.

Exercise: Healthy Steps

WHO: Solo

WHY: To notice the way we use our transitions at various times of day, and reflect on ways they might be channeled in service to our Intentions.

HOW:

Step 1 - Take a few moments to reflect on how we spend our time walking (or otherwise traveling) from place to place. In doing so, try to notice your pace, energy, and mindset as you walk:

- Am I rushing to this next meeting? What tension am I bringing to the meeting because of it?

Do I have an unresolved "bother" that I am now noticing as I walk, as it shows up in my tension and attitude? Do I have a way to put it aside so I can focus with full and best intentions and be present in my next interactions?

- Am I distracted by the beauty of the walk, taking me in a new, unanticipated direction that I actually appreciate more than my intended destination? What does that mean?

Step 2 - These are all useful things to notice: Consider other ways to demonstrate and practice "taking healthy steps" in this Journey, including non-physical ways so that this is a more inclusive and accessible practice...If it is helpful, write down these ideas to use later.

By slowing down, I tend to notice more.
By listening, I tend to understand the
Needs of others better.
By taking time, I get to
Meaningful Outcomes faster.

LESSON 3: RECONSIDER "TIME"

"The moment is simply structured that way."
- Kurt Vonnegut, Slaughterhouse Five (1969)

An element that distracts us from Intention is the fragmentation of the modern organization and the activities that support it: One meeting flows into another, each having limited relevance to the next, and the tasks that relate to each conversation get obscured by the urgency of recent calls to action. We are stressed by the mountain of unresolved conversations, often accompanied by vast amounts of time-wasting and sense-numbing mountains of data. We underutilize our talents and devolve into problem-solving approaches that often fail to produce viable solutions. And because bureaucracy channels our efforts in ways that make true connection across perspectives less likely, we often engage in "managing up/down" behaviors that are politically risk-averse, further hindering quality communication from occurring.

The poet David Whyte, who specializes in helping us make sense of corporate life and work through artistic reflection, has offered many writings on the subject of Time. This excerpt seems appropriate here:

Time is a Season

- David Whyte (2001)

Most traditional human cultures have seen the hours of the days in the same way as they have encountered the seasons of the year: not as clear lines drawn across our experience, but as an advancing quality, a presence, a visitation, and an emergence of something growing inside us as much as it is growing in the outer world. A season or an hour of the day is a visitation whose return is not always assured. Every spring following a long winter feels as miraculous as if we are seeing it for the first time. Out of the dead garden rises abundance beyond a winter eye's comprehension. The hours and the seasons are sometimes a flowering, sometimes a disappearance, and often an indistinguishable transience between the two, but all the hours of the day and the seasons of the year enunciate some quality in the world that has its own time and place. To make friends with the hours is to come to know all the hidden correspondences inside our own bodies that match the richness and movement of life we see around us. The tragedy of constant scheduling in our work is its mechanical effect on the hours, and subsequently on our bodies, reducing the spectrum of our individual character and color to a gray sameness. Every hour left to itself has its mood and difference, a quality that should change us and re-create us according to its effect upon us.[2]

Exercise: Time for Intentions

WHO: Solo

WHY: How do we approach Time so it flows in a manner consistent with our Intentions? Here is an exercise that helps us gain greater clarity:

HOW:

Step 1 - Recall a specific time when you were a member of a group that "flowed..." Time passed in a way that was scarcely noticeable, as you and others so cherished the work you were doing and the time you spent together that you gladly worked beyond normal time frames until exhausted but satisfied, you finally adjourned.

Step 2 - Journal this experience. Notice:

- What made this experience so memorable for you?
- How did you feel at the time?
- Are there any aspects of that experience that you seek to replicate today in your work?
- How do these insights inform your interest in focusing on What Matters consistent with your Intentions?

Practical Application of Intention - Link Time, Intention, and Calendar

What do I want to get out of that meeting? How does it relate to other things that matter? How does it help me (or not) in terms of my Intention for the day? One of the core tools we rely upon is our Calendar, but it often feels like the Calendar is dictating the terms of engagement, rather than serving our Intentions, Values, and project priorities. The "Desired Calendar" exercise brings these things into alignment: By creating a tool that allows us to clearly see What Matters, it reminds us of those things we intend to do before they are derailed by unexpected noise. It can also provide a way to reflect on what has actually been accomplished, which facilitates further planning around priorities.

The format is simple: **TASKS -> REFLECTIONS -> NEXT STEPS** are identified, all grounded within reminders of Intentions and Values. With practice, such a tool integrates into others you use routinely in your work, such as diverting certain email to a "To Be Read Later" folder, or combining certain documents into ad hoc folders that are used to manage the tasks of the day. You may integrate the Desired Calendar with a project management tool, such as a GANTT Chart, as well; *the point is that we are using our time in a manner consistent with our Intentions.*

Exercise: Desired Calendar

WHO: Solo

WHY: Create a Desired Calendar in support of efforts to clarify Intentions.

HOW:

Step 1 - At the start of the day, create your own "Desired Calendar" for the day. Using whatever technology suits you (paper, online calendar, phone, etc.), list and review the tasks you wish to accomplish today.

If you were to create an "agenda" of these items, identify specific objectives associated with each one - for today only - and the time likely needed.

If connecting with others is required, be sure to consider when in the sequence of task completion that is likely to occur.

Insert "project time" into your day, using your calendar to block it out.

Step 2 - Repeat this process each day for a week. Adjust in order to realistically fit your priorities and Intentions.

Intentions:

ACCOUNTABILITY: Being accessible and responsive, keeping promises

GENEROSITY: Seeking out others to understand their needs, looking for ways I can share knowledge and resources to support their efforts

PURPOSEFUL USE OF TIME: Maintaining awareness of time "frittering" or avoiding tough projects and conversations...staying disciplined to revisit Desired Calendar

TASKS →	REFLECTIONS →	NEXT STEPS
1. Write Friday presentation, confirm setup (45m) 2. Review notes from AZ, LW-B, ES - follow-up with BL (30m) 3. Review, confirm final arrangements for Thursday (60m) 4. Draft Tuesday work group agenda (20m)	1. Friday presentation says what is important, concisely 2. Defer reply to AZ... needs more thought. New note from SD also needs attention. 3. Note from SP was a surprise - glad I took time to respond! 4. All set for Thur/Fri - go! 5. Drafted Tuesday outline after good input from LW-B	1. Set aside time to finalize and print Friday presentation (60m) 2. Set aside time tomorrow for Tuesday presentation, print if possible. (60m) 3. Finish reply to AZ (30m) 4. Attend to SD note (30m)

Desired Calendar

Try to follow this approach as well as possible, inserting and deleting actions as the day continues. At the end of the day, review the actual flow of the day in comparison; learn from each day and continue to refine this exercise. Be sure to compare the activities with your Intentions for the day.

This entire process of developing and using a Desired Calendar may not be as poetic or philosophical as Whyte invites us to be, but it serves as a practical starting point from which deeper, meaningful reflection may be translated into practical actions. We call this Purposeful Work.

A Wandering: "Random Moment Time Studies, Competencies, Etc."

I think I'm going to let my mind wander awhile...

What is a "random moment time study?" I'm sitting in an agency waiting for a client meeting, and I notice warnings that all should monitor conversations because interviews for this study are taking place: Do caseworkers and bureaucrats contact unsuspecting random people to understand how they are spending time at the moment? Or are they connecting with people to see what type of time they are experiencing, and whether that is random or predictably sequential?

I'm reminded of Alan Lightman's memorable book, *Einstein's Dreams*, in which the properties of physics that Einstein discerned are applied to his dreams about the world in which he lived at the time he devised his Theory of Relativity. Lightman offers compelling chapters, each told in a different time relationship (e.g., accelerated, backward) for understanding the world... it's truly a wonderful reading experience.

But is this Random Moment Time Study (RMTS) a serendipitously wonderful encounter with Einstein? I doubt it. The bureaucratic culture of public agencies leaves little room for creative serendipity or wonderment of any kind. An RMTS is likely an effort to control random moments and reduce their occurrence. It is likely indicative of a delusional attempt to revive Taylorism in its Postmodern form, now ubiquitously framed as "Alignment Around Competencies that can Measure Engagement" within an organization. Well-intended perhaps, but delusional.

We often contemplate the urgency to "develop sound competencies" in our workforce, measure the success of training to achieve them, and therefore gear any and every teachable unit in that direction. I'm bored with such thinking. Yes, we can design training courses to have pre/post tests of knowledge, self-assessed and 'objectively' assessed results, etc. But it is the GESTALT of the holistic learning experience that matters, and the UNIQUENESS OF LEARNING IN COMMUNITY that discerns what we can offer from a routine, modular, technical training.

It's harder. It's more complex. It defies being easily REPLICABLE, though.

I have little quibble with some of the basic intentions around such things: Companies, non-profits, etc. must be 'stewards of our resources' and seek efficiencies towards effective customer service. Got it. But what bothers me is the ILLUSION OF CONTROL associated with such efforts, and the CENTRALLY HIERARCHICAL DECISION-MAKING AND REGULATORY STRUCTURE that arises from the illusion. This is a dated approach, and even in its heyday, it was based upon fallacies borne of Theory X management concepts.[3]

Others have seen this coming for quite awhile: So why are we still stuck in outmoded command and control approaches to management? In a Post-Industrial Society, as Daniel Bell prophesied 40+ years ago,[4] the exchange of information among all of us does not occur through a prism of Scarcity, but must open us to generously sharing tidbits from our varied perspectives through channels that more naturally arise. The 'market' in this case clusters around 'increasing returns' on the value of this information, as Brian Arthur well-articulated,[5] and the subsequent modeling on Network Effects demonstrates, and Scarcity as a justification for centralized control and resource alignment loses its credibility and utility.

People are complex beings. Organizations are complex entities. Beyond the mere commodity production of goods and services that can be readily manufactured and apportioned, most of the work of the human world needs to be understood through complex interactions that can only be temporarily understood, because they then morph and transform in different ways. While predictability is possible to some degree of certainty, the greater challenge is to EMBRACE THE ARTISTRY OF THE HUMAN CONDITION AND LOVE THE MOMENT AND ITS EPIPHANIES.

The Random Moment Time Study likely will not discover this elemental truth.

Do Purposeful Work by Connecting Intention to the Desired Calendar

The concluding step of this initial overview invites us to consider how we connect Values, Intention, and the Calendar that guide our work week. This integration allows us to focus upon Purposeful Work. **Purposeful Work is where our heads, hands, and hearts meet,** the place where "a good day's work" invigorates us and motivates us to sustain and persevere in the face of major obstacles. [6]

Purposeful Work is often undermined by a lack of wholeness: We generally fail to look at our work as an integrated set of opportunities to continue to a clear purpose where each activity is related to each other activity, where each thought can make a contribution to other thoughts that emerge in a complete and meaningful narrative.

Exercise: Purposeful Work - Connecting Calendar to Intention

WHO: Solo

WHY: A simple way to reveal Purposeful Work is to start with the Intentions of the day...

HOW:

Step 1 - Return to your Intentions that you set for today. Then look at the results of today's Desired Calendar exercise:

- How well did your day's activities align with your Intentions?
- How mindful were you of the meaning of your activities as you navigated the day?

Step 2 - If your work is so structured, expand this purview to the week, month, season, or year... just do what fits your own work.

Step 3 - Save the results of this exercise, as we shall use them later.

Intention helps us notice those things that matter, so we can transcend the systemic obstacles of our workplace cultures that inhibit us. It offers a good place to begin, a way to prepare to engage in the things that matter at work. But what really matters?

LESSON 4: CLARIFY INTENTIONS AND VALUES

The Core Story: Connect to Your "Why"

For what seems to be forever, people have been looking heavenward and asking, *"Who am I? Who are we? Why are we here? What is my role in that story?"* This is the Core Story, the ever-present narrative that runs throughout our lives. The Core Story is most prominent at times of transition: in childhood, as we transition to adolescence, and again as we fall in love and make deep commitments to our life partners. It is on our minds as we consider our careers, as well, if we are fortunate enough to contemplate the distinctions between jobs and work, between obligations to survive and opportunities to thrive. Such spiritual reflections also return at various pauses in the road, as we consider job changes or new career choices, or moving to new communities and the impacts on our families and relationships. And, of course, the Core Story is present as we age and contemplate the ends of our lives, now asking those same questions from the perspective of experience and, hopefully, some wisdom.

In his engaging books and talks on the topic, Simon Sinek asserts that our Core Stories need to *"Start With Why,"*[7] rather than our usual patterns that start with What we do and How we do it. "Why" is at the core of our purpose, the way we reveal the vast meaning of our Intention in the world. For some of us, the Core

Story is huge in scale and ambition, like seeking to eradicate poverty. But for most of us, it revolves around our more immediate circles of influence, such as our family and community. In a workplace context, the Core Story arouses our passions to produce an outstanding product of great value to others, or to deliver a service that recipients regard highly and that our colleagues tremendously respect.

Exercise: Your Core Story

WHO: Solo/Pair

WHY: What do you currently understand to be your Core Story? One way to access this information is to consider WHY you are living your life, your deeper sense of Purpose. Then you consider WHAT you have done or planned to do in order to fulfill this purpose, and finally HOW you try to engage in activities that support what you do and why you do it.

HOW:

Step 1 - Find a space where you can take time to reflect, journal, paint, or otherwise clarify your Core Story as it now expresses itself. We are all "works in progress," so please try not to expect perfection... this is a first draft.

Step 2 - Discuss your responses with a trusted friend or colleague. (Indeed, you may both do this exercise and share your stories with one another).

Step 3 - Reflect more fully on the connection of your activities to your Purposeful Work (Lesson 3) and your own evolving Core Story: What does it tell you? What might be meaningful to incorporate into your day, or at least into some aspects of your week?

These initial concepts and exercises are all about preparation, so we may greet the opportunity of our work with clarity of purpose and tools that support this clarity. We now need to anchor such preparation in What Matters.

Core Values: Keys to Navigating What Matters

The Core Story helps us discern the Values that form the foundation of our Intention. For me, a few of these have emerged that seem to relate to both my personal and professional lives. For you, there may be others that are most important. The key is to engage in the reflection and then use what emerges as a guide to your own Intention. Some that matter to me include:

Gratitude

I find it beneficial to remind myself that I am grateful for my Life, for my Spirit, for my Consciousness, and for the people who love me and help fulfill the purpose and opportunity of life. By regularly focusing on Gratitude and expressing it aloud, I am reminded of the precious and fragile nature of our lives and of the special privilege before us to use this life in service to others and to the Earth.

Integrity and Trustworthiness

You should know with confidence that if I promise something to you, I will do my utmost to deliver on that promise. I will also honestly point out concerns to you, those behaviors and ideas that I can plainly see will likely cause difficulties in our efforts to focus on What Matters. Trust is actually a really complicated concept, interpreted quite differently across situations and cultures; we will return to it in greater depth later.

Transparency

Responsible transparency helps us bring our best collective resources to the challenges that face us. When workers, managers, and customers all reliably know that the full story is being revealed and the implications of various options, decisions, and policies are being forthrightly discussed, the consequences for the organization are manifestly improved. Transparency can be at odds with confidentiality and the readiness to share information – such tension is natural. But if we start from this value, we can generally insure that all stakeholders in an issue are able to share their perspectives regarding who needs to know, what they need to understand, and how such things should be conveyed.

Compassion

We all better serve one another if we take the time to slow down, notice those among us experiencing pain, trauma, and loss, and extend ourselves to one another with compassion. This does not mean that we rescue each other from sources of pain and struggle, or engage in dysfunctional enabling behaviors that foster poor practices. But it does mean that we connect, we listen, and we seek to accommodate our organization's practices to allow our staff and customers the chance to face personal challenges (illness, divorce, financial strains, etc.) with dignity and respect.

Inclusivity

We are all so much better when we are genuinely capable of welcoming all voices and perspectives to a challenging conversation: We learn about the impacts of ideas and decisions that otherwise elude us, we witness new ways of seeing, knowing, and being that would never be noticed, and we hear potential solutions that would never otherwise be raised. Inclusive workplaces genuinely strive to create such consultations as routine, pragmatic expressions of diversity, going far beyond a simple invitation to "join us" to being a space explores shared meaning.

Tolerance for Ambiguity

I recognize that in a diverse, multicultural, multi-linguistic world, there will be a number of regular occurrences in which I am challenged to figure out what is going on, and why people hold the perspectives they hold regarding a given situation. My ability to be flexible in such situations is rooted in a value of tolerance for ambiguity, where I respect and seek these perspectives and my own biases about them before rushing to judgment and action. This can slow down decision-making, to be sure, but I'd prefer to slow down, understand what I don't know, and then get to the right decisions as a result. This means being OK with the ambiguity, even welcoming it, so we can collectively "work smarter" in the end.

The Coat of Arms: Representing Our Core Values

For centuries, families, governments, and companies have represented their essential qualities and values through a Coat of Arms. While rooted in feudal military history, this tool has been readily adapted to illustrate to the world those things that matter, how we wish to be known, and a legacy to future generations of our family. Combined with a Motto, we capture our values artistically and elegantly.

Exercise: Coat of Arms

WHO: Solo/Pair

WHY: What are your Core Values? To what degree do they consciously guide your Intentions? This exercise is a creative way to find some answers.

HOW:

Step 1 - Take a few minutes to reflect on these questions. Then briefly illustrate your responses, using the Coat of Arms Worksheet provided in Appendix B (or making a copy to complete separately).

Step 2 - Once completed, return to the last exercise and your emerging Core Story. Is there now more that you can say about it?

Step 3 - Meet with the Partner identified in the previous exercise. Share your Coat of Arms and the meaning it has for you.

In each box, represent a value that matters to you in your life and work. It may be a picture, phrase, or other artistic representation. At the bottom, insert a simple Motto that captures the essence of the values that guide you.

LESSON 5: FROM BELIEFS TO BEHAVIORS

The Core Story is an excellent foundation to build upon, but in the workplace we must ultimately deliver results. How do we apply our Values to the right areas of focus? How do we act effectively to achieve great results?

In my consulting and teaching, I have often found it helpful to share this diagram:

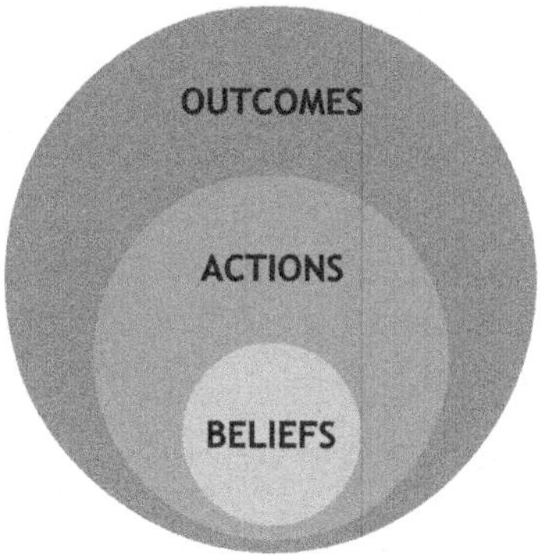

From Beliefs to Outcomes

Our core BELIEFS are formed early in life, and they filter our attitudes regarding the various situations and challenges we face. As such, we may be optimistic or pessimistic about what is possible, whether change can be beneficial or threatening, and what our priority values may be regarding a given project. But if we can focus on ACTIONS, there is room for experimentation: Asking the question, "In what ways might we do..." opens us up to alternative results and outcomes without necessarily threatening our underlying beliefs about the system or culture in which we are operating. This question is often extremely helpful at times of stress, conflict, or resistance to changes being contemplated; rather than starting from, "Your beliefs are wrong. Here is the right way to see things," we can say, "It feels like people are expressing concerns about the consequences of the current process. How else might we approach the situation?"

If we clarify our Values, as we have done these past few activities, we can define the conditions that must be satisfied to reach milestones that matter along our Journey. By then prototyping alternative actions as options, new OUTCOMES become possible.

Rolf Smith founded the Office of Strategic Innovation for the US Air Force, and has been a mentor to many others in the field of innovation. Smith offers an excellent framework for considering the range of actions we might take to move from Values to Actions and Desired Outcomes. His book, *7 Levels of Change: Diffferent Thinking for Diffferent Results* (3rd Edition, 2007) is essential reading that articulates this framework:

Level 1: Do the right thing. Focus on where you are supposed to be going. Anything else distracts us from the core goal. If you are not doing the right thing, you are doing the wrong thing.

Level 2: Do the thing right. Help people and systems work together as planned.

Level 3: Do things better. Continually improve on what exists.

Level 4: Do away with things. Eliminate anything that gets in the way of real work. Supplies, equipment, outdated policies, assumptions, etc. Become an "Essentialist," as Greg McKeown would put it.

Level 5: Do what others are doing. Copy proven processes, ideas from other industries, your own industry, you own organization. Become a cultural anthropologist, and "manage by wandering around" to find great ideas from what others are doing.

Level 6: Do what no one else is doing. Lead the pack in terms of innovative thinking. This requires revolutionary thinking. Combine two seemingly unconnected thoughts into one great idea, truly embracing "outside the box" thoughts and actions.

Level 7: Do what can't be done. Think the impossible and figure a way to refit it into reality. Weird thinking is required! (This is truly Six Sigma, if that strikes a chord with you.)

What should be apparent is that innovative approaches to change can be powerful at many levels. Perhaps Level 1 or 2 are most important to you right now; just focus on the right thing and to stop doing things that are destructive and wasteful can be timely, practical, and useful. Others may be in a very different context, needing to disrupt traditional approaches and take a fundamentally different attitude towards deeply entrenched processes. Either way, use your Values to set the proper course to notice What Matters.

Exercise: Align Values, Behaviors, and Desired Change

WHO: Solo/Pair/Group

WHY: To move from what we believe to behaviors that Matter, using insights from Smith's "7 Levels of Change" model.

HOW: Start with a blank sheet of paper or a simple spreadsheet. We have provided the "7 Levels of Change" Worksheet in Appendix B.

Step 1 - Using results from previous exercises, write your Core Values across the top. Notice Smith's "7 Levels" down the left side.

Step 2 - Using the cells created by points of intersection, enter Actions that can be taken that align values and levels of change.

Step 3 - Consider:

- What's emerging for you?
- Where do you notice repeated Actions that seem to Matter at this time to you and your organization?

Step 4 - Discuss the results with a colleague (alternatively, this can be a group exercise). What are some Desired Outcomes that appear as a result of this initial thinking?

Step 5 - Save these results - we will engage in later activities that can build upon this work. Smith's book is also a great resource here, offering activities at each level.

Let's return to T. S. Eliot's poem, *Little Gidding,* to summarize our work thus far:

"...With the drawing of this Love and the voice of this Calling
We shall not cease from exploration
And the end of all our exploring
Will be to arrive where we started
And know the place for the first time.
Through the unknown, unremembered gate
When the last of Earth left to discover
Is that which was the beginning;
At the source of the longest river
The voice of the hidden waterfall
And the children in the apple-tree

Not known, because not looked for
But heard, half-heard, in the stillness
Between two waves of the sea..."
- T. S. Eliot, Little Gidding (1942)

May the Journey continue...

LESSON 6: LISTEN WITH HUMILITY AND CURIOSITY

"We must become better at asking and do less telling in a culture that overvalues telling." - Edgar Schein, Humble Inquiry (2014)

We constantly communicate, but do we truly understand one another? Much conflict occurs because of misunderstanding, and as we engage in hurried, often remote communication strategies, we tend to hear only part of the situation. We then affiliate with those we perceive to be similar to us and "on our side" of the work issue, or become further entrenched in the social or political divide. This is not a recent phenomenon, as there is often a deep suspicion of Other that expresses itself across cultures and centuries (this is further discussed in Lesson 18 on Diversity and Inclusion).

Today's workplace requires us to pay attention, communicate effectively, and work collaboratively to address complex issues. Yet because we are overwhelmed with information and have difficulty discerning where to focus our attention, it is easy to get lost in the minutiae and lose What Matters. We need to listen... deeply... and we need to be fully Present to the Core Story, Values, and Intentions that should be guiding our efforts and those of our colleagues.

Management guru Edgar Schein offers an important set of insights in this regard: Through his books, *Humble Inquiry* (2014) and *Humble Consulting* (2016), Schein recognizes that those with the privilege of position and power often miss what needs to be learned from their colleagues, due either to perceptions of 'normal behavior' or arrogance. He argues that many errors in judgment and decision-making could be avoided with a fundamental shift in attitudes by such leaders, accompanied by a commitment to fully listen to one another. He calls it, "humble inquiry." I see it as a combination of humility, curiosity, and openness to diverse (and divergent) perspectives in our pursuit of What Matters.

Listening fully must be accompanied by a commitment to ***really learn from one another*** through our conversations. All too often, consultants, technical experts, and those in leadership roles are expected to have the answers. Yet much of the knowledge required comes from others, across the organization, perhaps with unassuming titles. This takes a little more time in the near term, but in the long run it yields vast dividends of insight, understanding, and focused action in pursuit of the right solutions to correct problems.

We focus here on the simple act of listening, which encourages authentic communication around meaningful issues. Through such conversations, relationships are built and insights into our Core Stories are developed, all benefiting from a genuine sense of curiosity and openness.[8]

Exercise: Listen with Humility and Curiosity

WHO: Solo/Pair

WHY: To have a meaningful conversation, characterized by deep listening, humility, openness, and curiosity, in order to foster effective mutual understanding. From resulting insights, participants may best determine what actions, if any, are required.

HOW: You will need a Partner for this activity... perhaps someone already involved in your efforts at What Matters at Work... or it could be a colleague you don't know as well.

Step 1 - Be seated comfortably so you can easily see and hear your Partner. Take a deep breath, relax, and focus on your Partner in this conversation. Regard the other person with warmth and respect.

Step 2 - Take a listening stance, with an open body, removing distractions. Invite your Partner to speak openly and honestly about a matter of personal importance to them, including how their experience has led to this perspective. Listen fully: As you do so, encourage, clarify, summarize, validate - demonstrate your humble curiosity without judgment. Allow sufficient time, at least five minutes.

Step 3 - Take a minute to inquire, "How might I be able to assist you?" The response from your Partner may be to simply be present and listen, or to ask your advice and guidance... that need comes from your Partner. If invited to do so, offer your guidance clearly, empathically, and concisely... speak from what you know, rather than to speculate or be judgmental. The Intention is for you to convey your full commitment to understanding your Partner's experience and truth, and to support your Partner's efforts to clarify What Matters as it emerges.

Step 4 - In turn, share your perspective on something that matters to you, perhaps from your Core Story. If your Partner can reciprocate your behaviors, you will both be able to benefit from such a conversation.

Step 5 - After the conversation ends, take a moment to reflect:

- What did you appreciate about this conversation?
- How might it have been improved?
- How might such conversations benefit us in our workplace?
- Are there opportunities to have them, or are there chances to create such opportunities?

Concluding Note to this Section

This is a good time to return to the results of the Purposeful Work activity (Lesson 3). Hopefully, there is now an emerging alignment among your Values, Intentions, Core Story, and activities. Sadly, for many of us, the discovery at this point is that there are vast "disconnects" among these discrete factors in our work lives. But this is fine: it helps us recognize more specifically the challenges we face and where we have energy to address those challenges.

In this first section, we have explored the underlying Intentions we bring to our work, begun to develop strategies for remaining true to those Intentions, and then connected these strategies to Values we hold deeply. All of this is integrated to form an emerging personal sense of purpose that guides us in our work. Much of this we call, "interior work," as we become more attuned to those inklings within us that are giving voice to What Matters. As we move forward to explore the terrain of our organization, look for ways it might support creative, meaningful work within healthy, sustaining spaces. Hold the results of these initial explorations near at hand.

Survey the Terrains of Organizational Culture

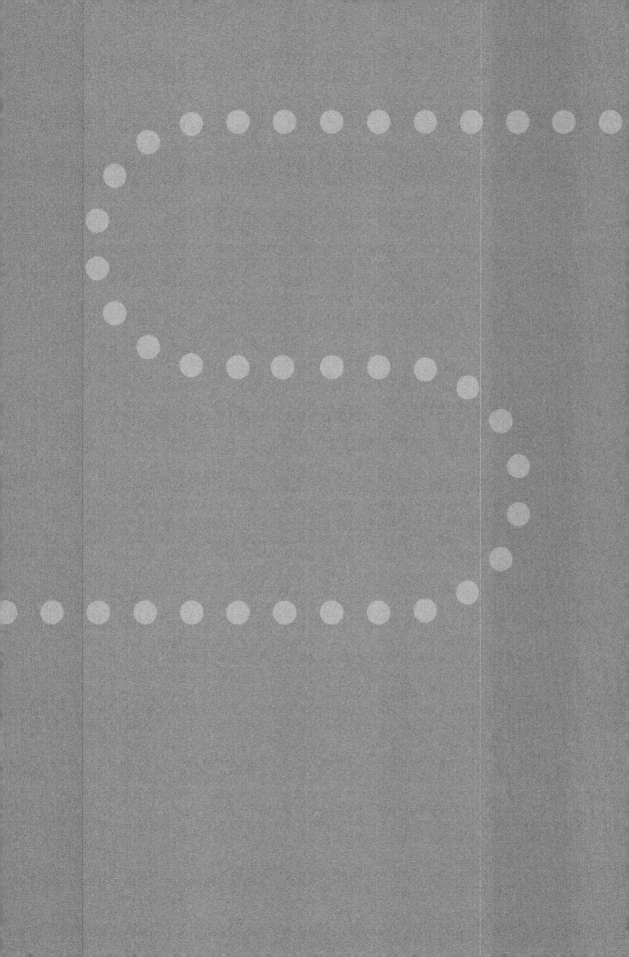

As we begin our Journey to accomplish What Matters at Work, we need to take stock of the territory we will encounter. These lessons focus on such matters, in turn focusing upon Communication, Decision-Making, Technology, Transparent Infrastructure, and Physical Space. While much of the preparation in the previous lessons was achieved independently, much of what now occurs must be done in partnership with fellow Journeyers - this is ultimately a "group experience" if it is to be successfully navigated. You will also notice a shift from your personal focus on What Matters to an emphasis on how the organization may align its structures, processes, and resources in this way.

LESSON 7: COMMUNICATE ACROSS THE ORGANIZATION

The effective flow of information is the lifeblood of the organization. Meg Wheatley alluded to it as the "circulatory system" or the bloodstream of the organism that is the modern company.[9] We need to make sure that information is getting where it is needed – consistent with our Core Values – and do so in a timely, accurate, and efficient manner that can be readily converted into productive knowledge.

Unfortunately, this is not the usual experience: Many staff complain that they don't receive what they need from managers or from across the bureaucratic abyss. Emails go without responses, decisions get deferred, policies and websites go without updating. People commonly complain they are "left out of the loop" and are thus left to make sense of what is happening with a lack of accurate information. As a result, customers are poorly served and the energy that could be channeled into effective problem solving and innovation goes wasted.

The 20th century organization emerged from concepts of bureaucracy and efficiency, where improvements were made upon the centralized hierarchies that preceded it. This concept was refined by ideas about mass production, with impersonal assembly lines for mechanical production and cubicle culture in drab offices. Information primarily flowed from the top down, within a strict reporting structure that reinforced the hierarchy of information and the power associated with it. It's debatable whether or not these innovations were fair, humane, or ultimately sustainable, but they dominated the capitalist landscape for over a century.

The 21st century company, however, has vastly different opportunities and requirements. As Rod Collins put it in his book, *Wiki Management* (2014), we now require a revolutionary model for collaborative management of organizations. The post-industrial Information Age in which we now reside allows and encourages information to flow up, down, and across complex networks that are largely unbounded by geography.

We need structures that facilitate communication in very different ways than those of the previous era. Integrating "high tech with high touch," as John Naisbitt expressed it forty years ago in his book, *Megatrends* (1982), is crucial to this transition. Naisbitt accurately foretold the need to dissolve hierarchical pyramid structures, replaced by networks as core organizational forms. But many businesses, public agencies, and other organizations are still stuck in the 20th century, and this is impeding their ability to innovate and their capacities to sustain necessary transformations of their business models.

The Internet has transformed information from being a scarce resource into one that is overwhelming and mind-numbing, where discerning that which we need to know or discard is the challenge of the hour. There are now highly different expectations regarding who "needs to know," what should be known, and the speed and privacy parameters with which it should become known. Thus, the old structures of hierarchy and approval continuously hamper our abilities to nimbly access the right information and share it in the proper forms with those who need it for their work.

I believe we now require significantly more democratic information and communication channels to facilitate rapid

knowledge-sharing and customer service. If we are to be true to our Core Values and Intentions, we need practices and structures that are built to support them. The directions and forms of communication flows cannot be overstated in their importance and centrality to our efforts. The mechanistic, hierarchical view of organizations served a different time and purpose, both culturally and economically.

Exercise: Communication in Your Organization

WHO: Solo

WHY: To map out the communication processes and structures, thus identifying strengths and weaknesses of the current state.

HOW: Use the Information and Communication Flow Worksheet provided in Appendix B.

Take a few minutes to outline the processes by which communication occurs as it flows through your organization (or the aspect on which you are now focused):

- Who's involved, and who isn't?
- What forms of communication are used, and what does that say about how inclusive communication is, or how power is shared and distributed?
- What does this tell you about the effectiveness of this communication for customers and employees, as well as for those in leadership roles?
- Are you all getting what is needed in a timely, useful, meaningful, and effective manner?
- When you examine your daily calendar, do you notice ways in which you might better support the type of communication that is required?
- Finally: How well does this analysis align with your Core Values?

LESSON 8: "DECISIONS, DECISIONS"

How are decisions made in your organization? Many organizations simply assume a hierarchical chain of command that is reflected in position power: Staff report to supervisors, who report to Directors, who report to VPs, up to the CEO. Decisions are made by those "up the food chain," and the jobs of those below are to comply and implement those decisions. We accept this structure and its natural consequences as if it were preordained by some inexorable power or divinity.

This approach persists despite well-known and understood realities of organization life:

- Decisions are often best made by those closest to the impact of the decision.
- Consultation and collaboration lead to better quality solutions to problems and decisions regarding those problems.
- Customers are best served when staff are empowered to quickly respond and address issues as they are faced.

What alternatives exist to this dominant model? While we could radically and fundamentally change decision-making through an approach like the Holacracy model (now famously implemented at Zappos Shoes, among other companies),[10] there are more incremental approaches that can be readily integrated into our current structures. A few considerations:

Decision-Making Methods

I like to consider a spectrum of decision-making options available to address any given issue. Over time, groups can readily discern the types of issues that are best addressed by a given approach, and place them in "decision baskets" so everyone transparently understands how they will be decided. Each method can have an appropriate application if wisely matched to circumstances and needs. For example, we might delegate technical decisions to specialists on a given issue, and they might seek consensus on highly important questions before acting upon them. On other questions, we might seek full staff advice, but after consultation a manager might make the decision. Teams need to assess the situation and consult with others; the choice of decision-making method is often a group's first important decision. By being transparent about which types of issues fall within each basket, trust and clarity are engendered. If issues arise that are beyond the anticipated sets of issues, there is a clear process by which such challenges are assigned to a basket for resolution.

We also need to create opportunities for groups to make their best decisions. This requires us to navigate what Sam Kaner calls the "Groan Zone,"[11] that phase of the process where everyone is so tired of deliberating that they want to give up and make a decision. But the Groan Zone is also an important learning opportunity, for it is through the strange ideas that come from unanticipated people, we find the nuggets that form innovative solutions. We must respect the capacity of the group to determine its best course of action, and by clarifying the appropriate approaches to decision-making around a given issue, channel energy more constructively and transparently.

METHOD	PLAINLY SPOKEN	STRENGTHS & WEAKNESSES
Autocratic	*"I am The Decider."*	S: Clear, efficient. W: Isolated from outside perspectives. Others may feel disenfranchised.
Consultative	*"What do you think? I want to hear from you before I make a decision."*	S: Clear, includes more perspectives, but still can be efficient. Increased ownership of decision. W: Consultations can go on endlessly and still people may feel excluded. Decisions can get lost among other priorities.
Persuasive Minority (Political)	*"We may be a small group, but we are influential and persistent."*	S: Passionate stakeholders are engaged and influential, so their interests are addressed...this can help with implementation. W: Majority views and expertise are excluded or overlooked.
Expert (Technocratic)	*"Let's use an expert panel and have them decide."*	S: Evidence-based decisions that are defensible and documented. More likely to be objective and have credibility, as such. W: Some may question biases and expertise, possibly feel some types of experience are excluded.
Averaging (Compromise)	*"Let's compromise and pick a mid-point."*	S: Efficiently moves forward on contentious issues. Satisfactory to most people. W: Perspectives remain positional, as underlying needs and concerns go unaddressed.
Majority Rules	*"Let's vote and let the majority decide."*	S: Clear, efficient, inclusive of all with 'standing.' Most people satisfied. W: Positions remain positional and minority may feel resentment.
Consensus	*"Let's talk things through until all are satisfied with the decision."*	S: Thorough, inclusive, focuses on underlying concerns. Often results in superior decisions and broad ownership to implement. W: Time-consuming. Can have "tyranny of mediocrity" shadow when some become exhausted with the process.
No Decision (Null)	*"Whatever happened? No decision seems to have been made"*	S: Whatever the natural consequences are, they happen. Those whose interests prefer no decision are satisfied. W: Many are dissatisfied and disillusioned, taking a toll on interest in future participation.

Decision-Making Methods

Exercise: Align Decision-Making Approaches with What is Needed

WHO: Solo

WHY: To clarify the current state of decision-making in your organization, from which we may explore other options.

HOW:

Step 1 - Identify "decision baskets" that readily batch various types of decisions into transparent processes for their resolution. Some decisions will be by consensus, some by majority rule, some by delegated and recognized subject matter experts (SMEs), some by those with hierarchical position power as managers, some independently by individuals charged with a scope of work.

Step 2 - Relate your responses here to those of the previous exercise regarding Communication: How might these two factors be addressed so that more transparent, inclusive Communication may be used to support effective Decision-Making?

LESSON 9: TECHNOLOGY WITH PURPOSE

Technology refers to more than the equipment, services, and resources available. It includes the array of capital equipment that may be accessed to facilitate production and service provision, the various ways information is stored and accessed, and how social media are utilized to communicate across the organization and with our customers. Technology resources should also support effective meetings through whiteboards, smart boards, flip charts, and movable furniture to facilitate effective conversations, as well as offering virtual meeting platforms.

At a very basic level, document sharing software that enhances collaboration has been integrated into our workflows. But we also require tools and virtual spaces that allow project team members to actively review, modify, and improve upon one another's prototypes until a best solution emerges. Platforms should facilitate such information sharing in an organic, largely democratic manner, as service providers consult with one another – and sometimes their customers – to solve problems and innovate on previous approaches. We need to take such concepts and scale them up to be accessible to virtually any stakeholder in a given aspect of company business, through a platform that encourages full participation within a responsibly transparent environment. Such approaches open up huge possibilities for creative, effective problem-solving.

How do we use technology in service to What Matters?

In their book, *Digital Habitats: Stewarding Technology for Communities* (2012), Etienne Wenger and his colleagues focus on how technology can be used in service to communities of practice and other collaborative learning enterprises. They offer a valuable set of practical inventories that can help us assess how well these technologies align with our priorities and goals, and whether they support the crucial community-building required. In addition to the activities being suggested here, we recommend that readers take a close look at *Digital Habitats* (especially the "Action Notebook," which contains those inventories for action) as an additional resource in this area.[12] Since so much of our work now occurs in virtual spaces, paying specific attention to how we best collaborate in such environments is essential as we translate our aspirations into meaningful actions.

Exercise: Mapping Technologies on our Organizational Landscape

WHO: Solo/Group

WHY: To clarify the various types of technologies available, how they are used, and how they serve What Matters.

HOW: Reflect on these questions and, as possible, engage colleagues with expertise needed for a meaningful conversation about them. As appropriate, download the *Digital Habitats* materials and incorporate them into your conversation.

- What is the role and relationship of technology to the overall set of communication, learning, problem solving, and decision processes of your organization?
- Who is engaged in assessing needs in this area, budgeting and prioritizing resources, and considering the diverse needs of various staff constituencies and customers that must be addressed?

LESSON 10: CREATE TRANSPARENT INFRASTRUCTURE

Infrastructure refers to those physical and virtual channels that exist to facilitate the productive flow of goods and services within an organization. These include communication channels needed to address important issues, production and distribution systems, decision-making channels, and financial flows.

Infrastructure connections may be seen as the "veins and arteries" of Wheatley's "circulatory system" referred to earlier.

Organization charts reflect aspects of infrastructure, but not the entire story: Much exists in the project teams, communities of practice, training resources, and technologies that are required to deliver services to customers. Transparency becomes an essential value of such infrastructures, facilitating the open sharing of information, decisional apparatus, and criteria for success.

As previously discussed, most 20th century businesses were characterized by control over information, so they created infrastructures intended to protect proprietary rights over that information. Security became paramount, and this is understandable. Yet 21st century organizations need to balance such protective structures and protocols with a significantly greater need for openness and transparency: Only through channels that facilitate idea sharing can the company respond nimbly to emerging opportunities and threats. Indeed, as well articulated in Brafman and Beckstrom's provocative book, *The Starfish and the Spider* (2006), centralized control can kill the responsiveness of the organization while decentralized infrastructures can facilitate its capacity to survive external attacks and threats to its viability.

Transparency is crucial to raise awareness and responsibility for external issues (e.g., climate change) that must become part of the conversation.[13] We can no longer ignore our global impacts; transparent infrastructures help us understand those influences by inviting diverse perspectives to come to bear witness, raise questions, offer new information, and help us responsibly respond to issues that arise from our production in the greater community. "Corporate Social Responsibility" can no longer be a vague concept, but one that incorporates environmental and social impacts that align with commitments to the traditional bottom line of economic measures. Transparent infrastructures are central to this arising concept, even integrated into "B Corp" certification[14] and related legislation.

This concern with infrastructure is essential to efforts that address complex "wicked problems" collaboratively (these will be discussed in Lesson 27), as well as to address other priorities in a way that includes all voices in policy development. If we are to achieve a "triple bottom line" (economic, social, environmental profitability), we require data that are often excluded from the conversation. For example, if we want to build a new service center across town from the current location, we may seek input from those who may benefit from the new location. But we should also hear from workers, customers, and community partners who may be upset by the change or displaced by the move, and understand community impacts from the traffic and environmental footprint of the new location.

Exercise: Assessing Infrastructure

WHO: Solo/Group

WHY: Infrastructure is an important aspect of our organizational terrain, but it is often less visible. This exercise is to make it more transparent.

HOW:

Step 1 - Consider the following questions:

- What structures exist within your organization to facilitate transparent collaboration and problem-solving?
- To what degree do security concerns inhibit the needed engagement of various types of expertise to address important issues, including those traditionally seen as external to organizational decisions?
- To what degree might you be able to influence the conversations needed in order to foster such structures being utilized?

Step 2 - Using a blank sheet of paper, create a Mind Map (a visual representation of the webs and connections that depict a given story) that shares the connections and activity centers that answer these questions.

Step 3 - As appropriate, involve a team with diverse perspectives on these issues in addressing the questions and developing the Mind Map.

Here's an example of a Mind Map to illustrate:

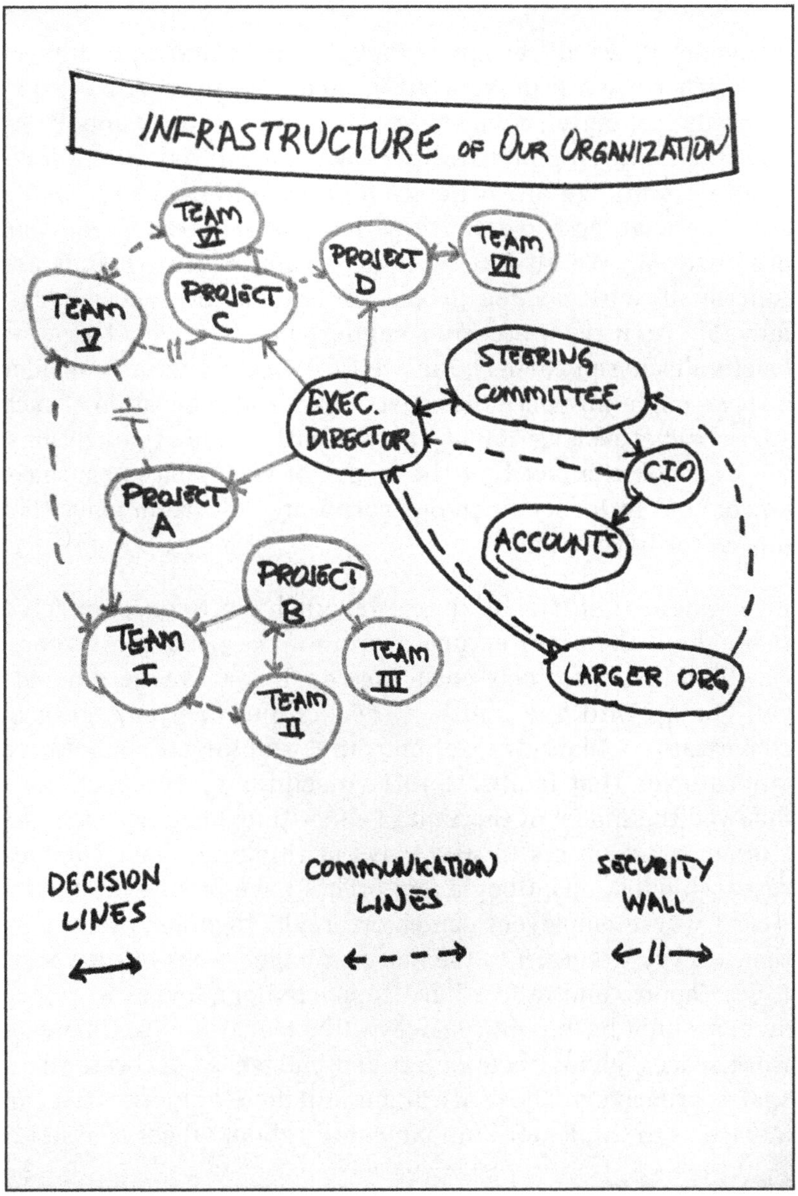

Infrastructure of Our Organization

LESSON 11: PHYSICAL SPACES AND RELATIONSHIPS

At one level, we all recognize that the space and environment in which we work make a difference. The presence of light helps us feel better, connecting to the natural world and lifting our spirits. Having private space we can call our own allows us to personalize our offices, cubicles, and desks to have a sense of meaning and identity within a large, often impersonal organization. We also know that certain meeting rooms are functional, with needed projection equipment, whiteboards, movable furniture, etc. that support effective meetings (as briefly discussed earlier). But we rarely take time to consider how we might influence the construction and renovation of such spaces, wherever we might operate within our organizations. We overlook the fact that the layout of such spaces can have a profound influence upon our corporate culture in ways that impact the bottom line.

Fundamental shifts in space design have been occurring throughout the architectural world for the past thirty years. New buildings routinely encourage open spaces where people can "bump into one another," serendipitously engaging in conversations that advance innovative thinking. Collaborative laboratories that facilitate inter-disciplinary research have followed the model of the Santa Fe Institute, opening scientists and social scientists to new ways of thinking about complex research questions. Google and others have pioneered playful spaces where employees can enjoy breaks together, recharging their energy to return to the more mundane tasks of their jobs. IDEO, Zappos, and others have supported employees in taking ownership of both public spaces – like elevators – and private work spaces, giving them power and budgets to decorate those spaces creatively. These are all helpful developments that can inspire us to think more fundamentally about what is possible.

At the Boston-area firm, *Humanyze*, they have explicitly taken such considerations about space into account:

> *"If you create an environment where random people bump into each other, then every so often pretty amazing things will happen,"* says their CEO, Ben Waber. *"It's building those levels of trust so the right stuff can happen more frequently."*

Humanyze analyzes workplace interactions, and has seen a direct relationship between architecture and increased business as a result.[15]

Such innovations in the design of physical space address another challenge of 21st century life: Paradoxical Loneliness. It is ironic that in this highly connected society, we are witnessing significant mental health and social issues related to being separated from one another, reinforced by cultural and political tribalism. Whether we are citing articles from years ago or more recent studies with an emphasis on internet-related issues,[16] we know this is a pervasive problem of modern life. But it appears to be exacerbated by our current technological addictions to social media that drive us into our own separate chat rooms, both at work and at home. Furthermore, our social media tends to further polarize us into tribal "echo chambers," that influence our capacity to understand and respect diverse perspectives and even the validity of the information upon which those views are developed.[17]

The impacts on our political life are well-documented – but what does this mean for our work lives? When we combine such technological factors that enhance Paradoxical Loneliness with the physical spaces that reinforce such separation, the necessary relationships and trust required to debate serious alternatives is inhibited. We focus on our own routines and those shared by others in our sphere of influence. The problems we face tend to only receive consultation from others with similar backgrounds, from our own departments, disciplines, and teams. For example, "Sales" staff are commonly separated from "Pre-production/Creative Services" staff, who are separated from "Production" staff in the process of developing and delivering a given project. Such separation is common practice, reinforcing our lack of understanding one another's cultures, decisional processes, project priorities, etc. This frequently leads to conflicts, frustrations, and much wasted effort. When trust devolves and communication breaks down, the organization often responds by creating "work around" efforts that reinforce the separation.

How do we get at What Matters regarding physical space?

It seems to boil down to a few simple principles:

Form Follows Function

The old adage still applies, yet is so often overlooked. Staff should work in spaces that are suited to their jobs, *as those jobs aspire and intend to be* rather than what has always been done in the past. If we are moving to "centers of excellence" in serving customers, people who staff those centers should be physically accessible to one another. If someone's work is more confidential or requires private space to think and work, be sure that person has ready access to such space as a routine part of the work day (it doesn't have to mean an exclusive private office, but it should include such space in a coordinated, predictable way rather than by hoping a conference room or "swing office" happens to be available). Think through the true priorities of any given position as a unit, and look for opportunities to modify position descriptions if we simply do not have the space to support them as currently designed.

Space Reflects Mission

Using education as an example, schools and universities of the 19th and 20th centuries were premised upon modes of teaching and learning that have given way to new visions and approaches. Today's students must learn how to collaborate, work in teams, and apply technical knowledge to complicated and complex problems. Yet most classrooms are permanent lecture halls, and smaller rooms tend to be arranged to support presentations, rather than active engagement in problem solving and feedback sessions.

Today's health care facilities, to take another example, highly depend upon technologies that facilitate remote consultations among colleagues: Therefore, we must create more spaces that facilitate seeing and hearing one another, comparing visual diagnostic tools or even visiting patients in this manner. Hospitals and clinics cannot view such spaces as luxuries, but as essential elements to fulfill their purpose in society. We must engage in discussions within our own organizations, and work to modify our spaces to align with their missions.

Space Flexes with Task

Remember that old vacant lot on the corner, and how people would "cut through" and create their own, more efficient path to get to their destinations? People "cut corners" because the extra tasks that have been built into bureaucratic processes don't often make sense to them. Granted, some of these redundancies are truly safeguards that either protect us or ensure that all voices are heard before moving ahead, considering those diverse perspectives. But much of the time, when we are confronted with unnecessary barriers to meeting our objectives, we tend to look for how to use the resources we are allotted and achieve them.

We often just "settle" for what we've been given: That lousy conference room with the long table and no place to take notes is accepted as "all that's available" and we make do with it. Instead, we should consider replacing fixed "status furniture" with more flexible, movable furnishings that can be adapted to a variety of tasks and purposes. This concept can be applied to vast warehouses destined to be made into permanent offices; consider designating a number of "flex spaces" that can be reserved and modified (form follows function) to meet varied needs throughout the week. The "cabin principle" applies here (leave the space as you found it, and clean up after your work), and there can be a shared commitment to understand the various types of needs that are required and how best to address them as a company. Yet at the same time, preserve personal privacy and autonomy where it is most important, so staff can stay attuned with individual roles and priorities.

Space Nourishes Individuals AND Relationships

We tend to reward private offices and desired locations to those privileged by seniority and hierarchy. But we also need to consider staff needs for privacy as confidentiality, as well as access to those people whose relationships are critical to success. Whose jobs require private space? Who needs to connect with whom through the course of the day or related to certain projects? This principle works in concert with those previously stated, considering the entirety of the staff as a collective enterprise.

Peter Block *Community: The Structure of Belonging* (2009) goes even further:

> *"Community is built when we sit in circles, when there are windows and the walls have signs of life, when every voice can be equally heard and amplified, when we are all on one level - and the chairs have wheels that swivel.*
>
> *When we have an opportunity to design new space, we need the following:*
>
> - *Reception areas that tell us we are in the right place and are welcome.*
> - *Hallways wide enough for intimate seating and casual contact.*
> - *Eating spaces that refresh us and encourage relatedness.*
> - *Meeting rooms designed with nature, art, conviviality, and citizen-to-citizen interaction in mind.*
> - *Large community spaces that have the qualities of communal intimacy.*
>
> *The design process itself needs to be an example of the future we are intending to create.*
>
> *Authentic citizen and employee engagement is as important as good design expertise."*

I think that captures my sentiments well.

Exercise: Physical Space and What Matters

WHO: Solo/Group

WHY: To examine how our current arrangements and priorities around space either enhance or inhibit abilities to focus on priorities in our organization.

HOW:

Step 1 - Take an inventory of the physical spaces with which you and your colleagues engage in your work. Consider the four principles outlined above:

- How well do we utilize such principles in our thinking about these spaces?
- Where are there "easy wins" that might readily be addressed to improve our workplace effectiveness?

Step 2 - Consider, as well, more fundamental changes in the physical plant that could radically align your space with your company's mission and customer service goals.

Step 3 - Bring your impressions to a group that can offer other perspectives and feedback, leading to the following discussion question:

- How might we engage as an organization in a fundamental consideration of where we are located to do the work that matters?

Optional Activity: Draw a picture of an ideal workspace, one that helps achieve your goals and is consistent with your Intentions and Core Values. Imagine you now worked in such a space... Answer the above exercise as it might occur in this newly imagined space.

LESSON 12: "NEXT-STAGE" ORGANIZATIONS

Among the books we should consult in our quest for What Matters is Frederic Laloux's profile of emerging "next-stage" companies, *Reinventing Organizations* (2014). Laloux builds upon Ken Wilbur's Integral Theory, which shows how human cultures have integrated needed values, capacities, and behaviors in order to adapt to specific contexts and conditions over time. We are on the verge of a "second tier," Wilbur and others in this field argue, one that takes the learning of all previous experience and applies it to our complex, emerging challenges. Indeed, much of what we are describing here about What Matters connects directly to Integral Theory, as facilitation techniques offered here build from that work.[18]

Laloux brilliantly and lucidly articulates how many organizations can apply this theory to business practice, both for-profit and nonprofit, across diverse industries and settings around the world. He identifies several breakthroughs that are responsible for the success of these organizations:

Self-Management

How do we empower staff and customers to work directly with one another, unencumbered by hierarchy and bureaucracy? Indeed, how do we create organizational infrastructures that facilitate effective communication and decision-making?

Striving for Wholeness

How do we encourage all involved in our organization to be their true selves, dropping the "masks" we often wear that inhibit our talents from being expressed? Might we transcend our predefined roles to be genuine human beings with one another?

Evolutionary Purpose

What might happen if we drop the pretense that we can "plan" the future, instead allowing it to emerge in accordance with what needs to happen? How might we create an organization that serves a greater purpose than merely protecting those things we are afraid to lose?

Throughout his research, Laloux found that companies that had evolved to that "next stage" had embraced these breakthroughs. Their efforts were applied to all aspects of organization structure, decision-making, physical space, communication, etc... issues that align with our considerations about the territory of our Journey.

Exercise: Create "Next-Stage" Organizations

WHO: Group

WHY: Let's try to envision the "next-stage" organization we seek to become. This is best done as a team exercise, but it could also begin with your personal reflection and then become a conversation with one or more other people. I'll frame it here for 12 people, but a smaller group can make it work well.

HOW:

Step 1 - Think about the questions offered regarding Laloux's breakthroughs. Quickly brainstorm as many responses to any of the questions for 5m (or slightly longer if you prefer). Then select a few you feel are worthy of further development, either because you see clear answers or because they are important questions where answers elude you... it's entirely up to you. My invitation is to BE DARING... DON'T JUST SETTLE FOR THE EASY ANSWERS.

Step 2 - Form triads. Each person in turn shares an area of focus where you seek advice from the others. Share your challenge for 1-2 minutes, then listen to the feedback. After each person has had a turn, take a few minutes to integrate the feedback into your thinking:

- What questions now emerge?
- Where are you now seeking advice?

Step 3 - Form new triads (this can be done in a number of ways... Try to interact with those you see less often). Repeat the previous process.

Step 4 - Use some large Post-It Notes and place them on an open wall or whiteboard as categories: Self-Management, Wholeness, and Purpose. Building upon your insights from the previous conversations, use smaller notes to post ideas that are emerging. Each person is encouraged to share ideas, regardless of how well-formed they may be at this time.

Step 5 - After posting such ideas for 10 minutes or so, step back and review together.

- What ideas are generating the greatest interest and energy from the group?
- Which are worth discussing further, perhaps testing whether they might be worth trying?

It is from such conversations that great ideas begin.

Explore Pathways and Practices

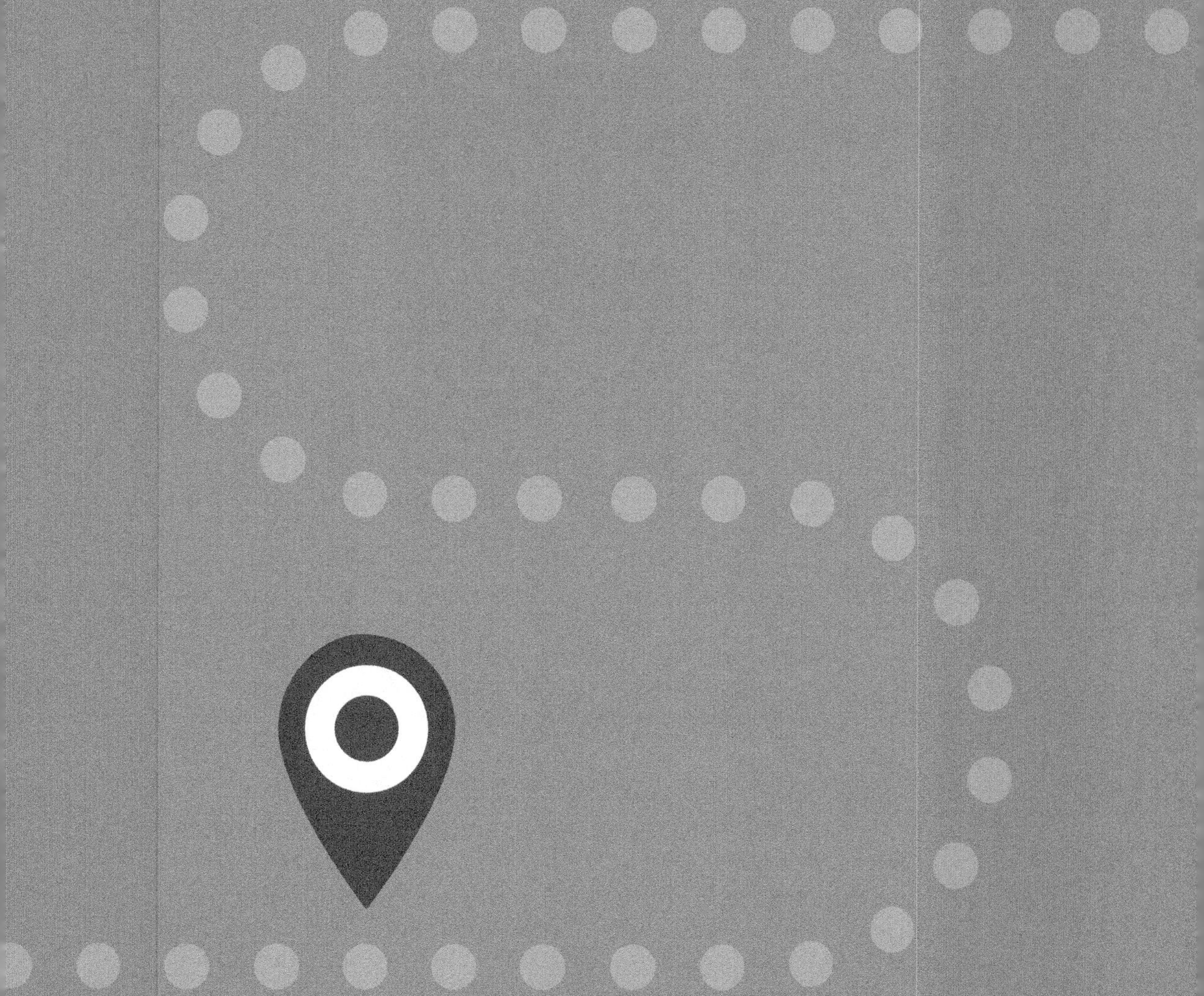

Outside Equator Coffee, Ottawa, July 2019

"If you don't know where you are going, any road will get you there!" - Cheshire Cat to Alice, Alice in Wonderland by Lewis Carroll (1865)

Now that we have surveyed the territory, we need to integrate understandings of best practices with tools for navigating its various elements. We need to consider the advantages and disadvantages of the paths that may be taken, as some may be easier but less sustainable, while others may be more challenging but ultimately reveal deep and meaningful results. We can apply our knowledge for facilitating groups to these opportunities and help us achieve what is otherwise unattainable.

These next lessons identify some of those practices and how they may be applied in practical and meaningful ways. Through these efforts, What Matters at Work becomes more clear to all on the Journey. While offered sequentially, they may certainly be taken in any order - it really does depend upon how you have engaged and responded to the challenges that have been posed in the first several Lessons.

LESSON 13: WELLNESS AND WELL-BEING

David Whyte has written extensively regarding the individual challenge of integrating identity with work and personal commitments. He speaks to this in his book, *The Three Marriages: Reimagining Work, Self and Relationship* (2009). Initially confronted with a request to speak about "work/life balance," he rejects that notion as overly simplistic and inadequate. Instead, Whyte invites us to regard three sacred commitments we make in our lives (my synthesis):

There is a commitment to Self, the vessel to nourish and sustain on the journey. This commitment has deep personal meaning and aligns with Intentions and Values, and is accessible to share through another person.

There is the commitment to Other, a life partner to share the journey. Much meaning is gained through the lens of the Other, who sheds light on aspects of ourselves we may be reluctant to notice and accept.

There is the commitment to Work. Far more than a job to get food on the table, Work is the synthesis of the intentions, values, and commitments made to Self and Other, and a "calling" to something greater than ourselves.

I find this approach to be beneficial in my own thinking: Rather than simply looking at how to "balance" my time, I think more holistically about committing to those relationships that matter deeply to me. Self, Other, and Work are integral to the overall sustainability and meaning of my Life Journey.

Keeping this in mind, we now introduce Wellness as a concept that offers several pathways and practices that may guide us well. The "Wellness Journey" offers highly accessible points of entry, so you and your team may readily choose what fits well with your Intentions, Values, and organizational culture.

Wellness and Well-Being as Core Commitments

In recent years, many organizations have jumped on the "wellness bandwagon," including an array of offerings: Wellness Committees sponsor potluck healthy lunches, exercise breaks, and onsite flu vaccinations, and company compensation packages include fitness memberships, reimbursed yoga and mindfulness classes, and incentives with insurance programs. These are positive steps, to be sure, but the Wellness Journey requires more.

In their path-breaking study, *The Healthy Company* (1992), Bob Rosen and Lisa Berger outlined several elements of the "healthy company" that had emerged from a decade of research across the world. Over the years, these initial concepts have been validated by additional research, and these "seven pillars of wellness" now guide much corporate thinking in this area. Here is one common expression of the approach, noted here in terms of personal wellness and well-being:

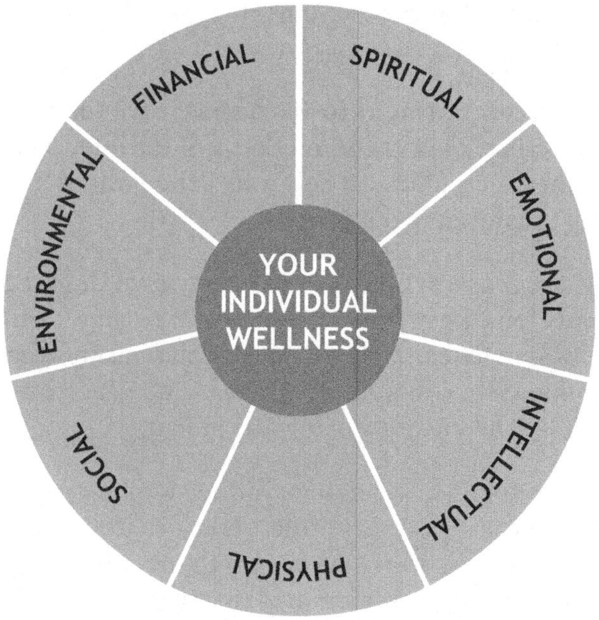

Wellness Wheel [19]

Spiritual wellness is a process of understanding beliefs, values, and ethics that help guide your life. Whatever your preferred approach, spending time asking and exploring your spiritual life can be an important part of your overall well-being.

Maintaining a **healthy emotional life** is important to overall health. Some ways to stay emotionally healthy are to manage your stress level, stay on top of work, get eight hours of sleep, and ask for help as it is needed.

Intellectual wellness means staying curious and engaged in learning new things. Engage in creative activities. Read for pleasure, be aware of social and political issues, or join a club that focuses on enhancing intellectual interests.

Physical wellness involves moving your body (exercise), eating well balanced meals (nutrition), sleeping, managing stress, receiving preventative care, and having routine health screenings.

Social wellness involves having a strong social network that can give you support and guidance when you are stressed or need stress relief. Additionally, these friendships can aid in developing and maintaining healthy relationships at various life stages.

Environmental wellness means taking care of your global environment and your personal surroundings. Declutter your workspace, take care of your home, contribute to the safety and beauty of your community - these are all ways to attend to your environment.

Financial wellness means taking steps to live within your financial means and planning for future financial health. You can do this by planning with a financial advisor, considering retirement planning as integral to life planning, and realistically looking at costs of housing, education, health care, travel, and other important aspects of your family's budget.

The challenge is to apply these concepts to the planning and execution of organizational decisions. However, this may appear to be at odds with the profit sought in the near term. For example, getting a new product or service out to customers in the fastest way may require long employee shifts and stressors that are contrary to health and well-being. But if we go a little more slowly, considering rest, exercise, and nutrition, we may reduce errors and notice risks. We thus reduce injuries and other mistakes, limit damage from poor decisions, and limit costs down the road. Manufacturing companies, for example, have celebrated "accident-free periods" for many years, and the commitment to safety is important. But they also need to look at underlying working conditions, and consider services that address mental health, substance abuse, and skills that may contribute to a sustained period of safety on the production line.

Looking at a related aspect, if we pay our workers well, including benefits packages and options that provide stability for their families, it may seem to negatively impact the bottom line. However, if doing so increases employee satisfaction, engagement, and retention, it has positive ripple effects throughout the surrounding community. By reducing gaps between top managers and line staff in compensation, as "Ben and Jerry's" famously did through their "compassionate capitalism" model, we improve larger social mobility outcomes as well![20]

Another important discovery of the Healthy Companies Foundation was how personal, "non-work-related" Wellness efforts relate to sustained workplace health. For example, if employees learn how to manage money well and address stressors related to their household budgets, it helps them focus more fully at work. If the company sponsors such opportunities through their HR or Employee Assistance efforts, this demonstrates appreciation and respect for the "whole person" and also contributes to employee retention and success.[21]

These are a few illustrations of how the apparent contradictions inherent in a Wellness and Well-Being commitment can be reconciled through understanding of our Core Values and Intentions, and how those insights can guide us in our planning and decision-making. These factors cannot be viewed in isolation. They are integral to our overall strategy and must be considered in developing priorities and allocating resources for learning and employee growth.

Exercise: Wellness and Well-Being

WHO: Solo/Group

WHY: To examine the realistic commitment of our organization to the principles and "pillars of wellness" so we may better understand strengths and weaknesses of current approaches.

HOW:

Step 1 - Consider the following questions:

- What does your organization claim to do in support of Wellness?
- How do these claims compare to actual practice, both in terms of core infrastructures and day-to-day work?
- What do employees need in this regard, and how do we know this?

Step 2 - Engage in some research regarding Wellness and Well-Being in your organization as it is experienced by your employees. A fun way to do so is to invite employees to cite examples of ways they promote their own Wellness, using the "seven pillars" as benchmarks. Staff can post pictures that illustrate these activities, either by their work areas or at a central location.[22] This visible statement, while not a scientific study, can reveal a great deal regarding how people interpret Wellness and the types of things they are doing.

Step 3 - Compare what is current practice to some of the "best practices" cited in the field.

Step 4 - Finally, consider how any of these approaches align with your Core Values.

In a recent *What Matters at Work* study group, one of the participants took the Wellness Journey to heart and introduced it to her unit. Her colleagues felt this was a key area they could act upon and, within a month, had made a commitment to this process: They began a series of "Wellness Coffee Conversations" that engaged many other staff across the Division. These actions quickly resulted in broader engagement and a yearlong Plan to explore the Seven Pillars through a diverse set of activities, all anchored in the monthly "coffee conversations." They connected with additional Wellness activities across the larger organization, which they leveraged into activities that benefited their units for very little financial commitment.

LESSON 14: FIND YOUR TRUE CALLING

In his influential book, *Good to Great* (2001), author Jim Collins shared extensive research regarding what really made the difference in facilitating the development of some companies from being merely "good" and profitable to being "great," vastly exceeding success metrics. He adapted the Ancient Greek Hedgehog Concept, where we focus on greatness in a specific area, and achieve it by focusing on three intersecting circles of activity:

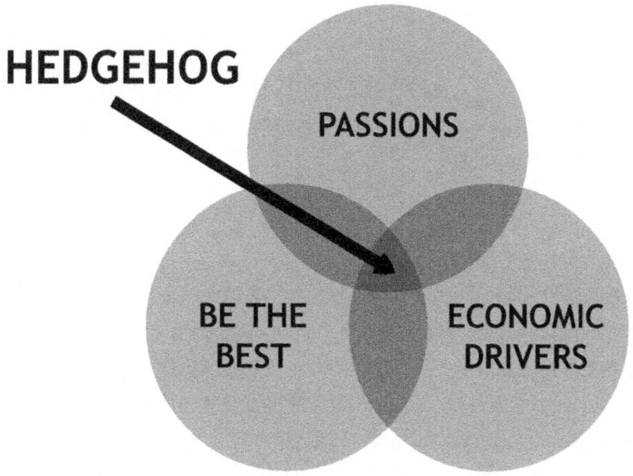

Hedgehog Diagram

- What are you **Deeply Passionate** about?
- What can you be the **Best in the World** at?
- What drives your **Economic Engine**?

These three questions are essential to uncovering our True Calling, where Passion, Talent, and Economic Sustainability conspire to breathe life into our efforts. Without such clarity, our organization will fall short of its true possibilities and we, as leaders and members of such companies, will be unable to sustain the energy required to live fulfilling, satisfying, engaging work lives.

So, how do we do it?

Exercise: True Calling

WHO: Solo/Pair

WHY: To clarify specific ways your work on What Matters connect to the things you feel "called" to do, with a sense of higher purpose and commitment.

HOW: This activity has two stages, each of which benefits from both personal reflection and partnering with a colleague for a peer coaching conversation:

STAGE 1

Step 1 - Draw your own "Hedgehog Diagram" using the three questions identified above. Individually, brainstorm a number of responses to each question. Be patient here - try to look at the question without being limited by your current role, situation, or career path... the Passion you have may relate to a field that is only beginning to emerge. *(On a personal level, I have fundamentally shifted career paths a few times, with satisfying results.)*

Step 2 - Then engage in a conversation with your WM@W Partner to gain a deeper understanding and appreciation of the possible responses, finally settling on one answer that is worth testing out for its potential value (a prototype).

Step 3 - Using this one answer, where your responses to the three questions intersect (a Hedgehog Response), engage in the second stage of the exercise.

STAGE 2

The second activity involves another tool, the GROW Diagram. GROW is a peer coaching tool utilized in many organizations around the world (you may already know it),[23] where the acronym means GOAL–>REALITY–>OPPORTUNITIES/OPTIONS–>WILL. (The GROW Diagram Worksheet is presented in Appendix B, where you will find a blank copy of the diagram, as well as possible coaching questions for your Partner.)

Step 4 - Complete the GROW Diagram and then discuss it with your Partner, where that person coaches you to consider how the Reality must be navigated to create Opportunities and Options to achieve your Goal, and ultimately to see where you have Will, or the energy to pursue a given Option. Ideally, you both complete the exercise and take turns coaching one another.

I have utilized these tools many times, in varied settings and contexts. I continue to be impressed by their capacity to inspire learners to be daring, to stretch beyond our usual expectations. Instead of thinking, *"What can I do to get by?"* consider, *"What am I passionate about doing that can have significant meaning in the world?"* With sustained commitment and the accountability of the peer coaching relationship, finding our True Calling can be one of the most important elements of the Wellness Journey.

I am also repeatedly impressed by the value of peer partners in such activities: Although our peers may lack any special expertise, or even have familiarity with the specific issues we are discussing, they often provide valuable guidance, clarity, and support as we wrestle with overwhelming challenges that have puzzled us. To have such colleagues and friends along this Journey can be immeasurably worthwhile, so choose wisely and be sure to thank them.

More Wandering: "Getting Lost in the Stacks"

For much of my life, going to a library meant fingering through the card catalog to find the appropriate book and its corresponding Dewey or Library of Congress number. I would then wander through the stacks of shelves, searching for the precise location of the intended book before resting upon the title. There was satisfaction in finding what was sought, to be sure, but there was deep joy that emerged from those discoveries that had not been anticipated: Alongside the titles that I knew in advance were others that I scarcely recognized, by authors unknown to me, regarding ideas that hadn't crossed my mind. Invariably, I would walk away with the book I had come to borrow, accompanied by three or four that now would occupy much of my reading time and interest. It always seemed to happen that way.

Today, we purposefully search titles on our phones, whether on the library site or Amazon, respond to suggested matches aligned with purposeful algorithms. We order our books with the full expectation they will be downloaded or delivered that day. We accomplish more in less time, to be sure, and we can access the information needed without much attention to geographic remoteness. Scans of eBooks and articles facilitate "open source" idea-sharing, and we needn't worry the book is "out of stock" for very long.

But there are trade-offs to accompany our modernity: We've lost much of the serendipity from the old library and book store experience. Those accidental discoveries had a timeless quality about them that I relish to this day. This is why I still love to wander into used bookstores, knowing full well that the title I seek may not be there. I can still get lost in the stacks, finger through shelves on topics I'd otherwise avoid, and get lost in the memories of other topics and conversations that weren't on my Agenda for the day. And from those memories, insights, and conversations I often find meaning that clarifies What Matters to me, deepening my commitments and my relationships. Sometimes, new Agenda items emerge in my core work, with greater value and more significant outcomes.

All from wandering in the stacks...

LESSON 15: CONNECT YOUR TRUE CALLING WITH LEARNING

"The most important investment you can make is in yourself." – Warren Buffett

Once we have clarified our True Calling and connected with our Intention, many of us ask, "So how do I acquire the skills and knowledge required to advance in my work?" and "How do I gain support from my supervisors for the learning I need to do?" As investment guru Warren Buffett has repeatedly emphasized,[24] YOU are the key asset here. So investing in your professional development becomes an essential element in the What Matters journey. One practical tool for articulating responses to these questions is the Individual Development Plan (IDP). While the IDP may be best utilized within an organization already committed to professional growth of employees, the IDP offers great benefits to individual employees seeking to discover What Matters at Work. There are numerous examples from industry and academia, and they tend to follow similar processes:

Assess Your Current Situation: What are your current roles and responsibilities? What skills and credentials do you possess that are being applied in your job?

Identify Possible Desired Directions: Where do you want to go? What is appealing about this direction?

Consider What You Need to Get There: What skills, experience, and credentials do you need to go in this direction?

Develop a Prototype Plan of Action: There may be several pathways to success. Consider them and prototype one or more – What resources exist to support your professional development and achieve this goal? How long will it take to find this position or develop this skill set?

Consider Short/Intermediate/Long Term Goals: Develop a plan that has six-month objectives, 1-2 year objectives and longer time frames... what is reasonable varies from field to field.

Identify "Next Steps": We all have to start somewhere... be sure you have a place to begin that is reasonable for you, considering your time, resources, and the real "terrain" of your support systems.

This process is best achieved with a Partner, and often it is useful to work with a professional coach or mentor to understand the array of resources available to you. Many of the initial responses to these questions can be gleaned from the GROW exercise we previously completed. This exercise is the next step along the Journey.

Exercise: Individual Development Plans

WHO: Solo/Pair

WHY: To connect True Calling with specific professional development plans that can serve as a map for your journey towards What Matters.

HOW:

Step 1 - Use the Individual Development Plan found in Appendix B, which has been adapted from a template used at the University of California-San Diego. Complete the first page, which may take 15-20 minutes. Pause for the next Step. Later, return to complete the IDP.

Step 2 - Partner with a colleague, perhaps your GROW peer coaching partner, to explore the results of the IDP exercise thus far.

Step 3 - Complete the rest of the IDP. As helpful, meet again with your Partner.

Step 4 - Consider:

- What appear to be useful "next steps" that have emerged?
- Where do you have the best opportunities to negotiate for support from your organization to engage in such learning?

There is no "right pathway" here, but awareness of both short-term and intermediate-term goals, resources, and specific action steps is timely at this stage of your experience. Honestly consider where you have current skills, resources, and credentials, as well as the requirements for gaining the knowledge needed to achieve your goals. The IDP becomes a road map that can be tweaked and improved over time.

LESSON 16: LEARNING AS A KEY PATHWAY

Let's zoom out again, taking into account the entire team, department, or organization that is your area of focus in this learning experience. Professional development offers a critical pathway to success on this Journey. In *The Fifth Discipline* (originally published in 1990), Peter Senge captured the essential competitive advantage required for the 21st century organization: We must cultivate learning organizations that continuously improve the capacities of employees, applying their knowledge to key challenges.

This guidance is as important today as when Senge and his colleagues first offered it thirty years ago: We know that employees given meaningful career development opportunities are much more engaged in their work and more likely to be retained by their organizations. Even if they take their skills elsewhere, they speak highly of their previous employers in this regard, enhancing the reputation of the company as a place to work. As a practical matter, such employees bring flexible thinking to complex challenges and to groups that must engage in breakthrough thinking. Because of this investment in learning and growth, the culture of the organization is more likely to experience a "tipping point" that allows transformation.

Learning and growth should not be limited to formal classes and workshops. Indeed, the largest percentage of time in this area should be focused on applied learning in the contexts that matter, with coaching and feedback regarding specific applications. In addition, we should create opportunities to share in face-to-face sessions and less formal settings, and through blog posts and articles that invite further comment. We should also develop "learning transcripts" that can benefit employees as they seek advancement opportunities. If managers build such thinking into performance management and goal-setting, they can mentor employees in choosing best pathways for career advancement.

The investment in learning needs to be connected to growth at several levels, including:

Level 1: Individual development of job-related skills, where there is a direct correlation to increased capacity to flourish in the current position. This includes onboarding, peer coaching, processing learning with experienced colleagues, and direct connection to performance management processes. By assessing skills routinely, staff can be credentialed to play leadership roles preparing other staff, as well;

Level 2: Individual development of broader skills, where there is a direct correlation to increased capacity to flourish in the current position. This includes onboarding, peer coaching, processing learning with experienced colleagues, and direct connection to performance management processes. By assessing skills routinely, staff can be credentialed to play leadership roles preparing other staff, as well;

Level 3: Team development that enables group members to function more effectively together, so they can discover both their strengths and natural sources of tension and conflict. Such efforts can include participation in StrengthsFinder,[25] the Myers-Briggs Type Indicator, DISC, and similar tools, then carefully integrating the insights gained into modified team practices - it does little good if we don't apply what we learn here!

Level 4: Organization-wide learning, where a conscientious effort is made to instill common cultural values, language, and processes and where sharing across units is encouraged. As Leaders embrace the concept of a learning organization, the message will be credible when managers discuss such efforts as part of their supervision. These need not be glitzy, expensive programs, but they should become routinely offered and valued, consistent with the values espoused and support the actual mission and work in which staff are engaged.

Exercise: Promote the Learning Organization

WHO: Solo/Pairs/Groups

WHY: To better understand the ways your organization supports efforts to fully develop its employees, both professionals and personally.

HOW: How does your organization promote learning and growth? To what degree is there support to apply what has been learned in such settings?

Step 1 - Take some time to reflect on these questions and to discuss them with relevant leaders, supervisors, and staff.

Step 2 - Interview at least three colleagues (preferably from diverse perspectives) regarding how they see such investment occurring in your organization.

Step 3 - Map out the results of your conversations (perhaps with a Mind Map), so you have a tangible product of your efforts.

Step 4 - Then: Look for ways to strengthen learning opportunities in a cost-effective manner that allows learning to be shared, applied, and evaluated in terms of your Core Values.

LESSON 17: THE LEARNING ORGANIZATION AND "ENGAGED PEDAGOGY"

The idea of the Learning Organization is easy to grasp, but challenging to implement. We aspire to have workplaces where there is an ongoing exchange of ideas, one where people learn from one another and apply that learning collaboratively and generously to challenges they face. But in order for that to occur, the ways we facilitate teaching and learning must be carefully crafted.

Learning is enhanced by genuine participation, supported by an affirming environment that catalyzes innovation and welcomes questions, doubts, critiques, and ideas that emanate from the 'edge' of the organizational: "Engaged Pedagogy." Rather than relying upon traditional training approaches, with vast periods of lecture punctuated by occasional discussion, we must actively engage learners with the material. David Kolb's *Experiential Learning Model* (1974) offers an excellent approach that has been applied to many types of settings, building from its core elements:

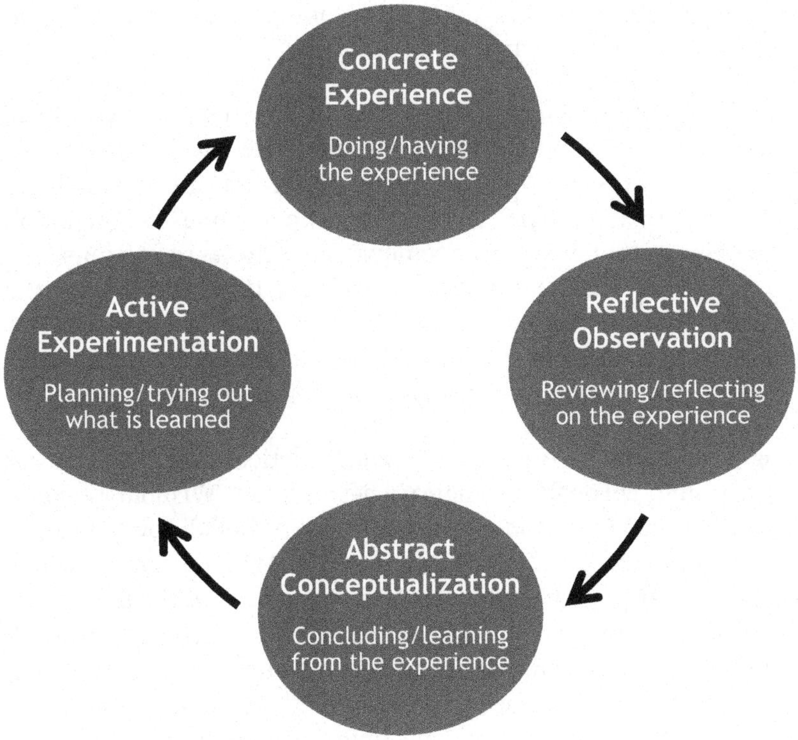

Kolb Learning Cycle[26]

By immediately engaging participants in the experience, they reflect upon how it relates to what they have previously learned or assumed. Reflection links the experience to abstract concepts and questions, such as "How might this be applied in my work setting?" If we provide concrete practice opportunities using realistic scenarios, learners can immediately test various responses to such questions.

Notice how this method flies in the face of traditional teaching/learning approaches: Rather than learners passively receiving content, mulling it over, and considering how to practically apply it, they are immediately thrust into the "stretch zone" of practicing the skills required to make important connections to what they already know and do. Teachers can immediately witness this effort and adjust their approaches to what they are now hearing, students can readily see what is clear and where they are confused, and "teachable moments" naturally emerge from the collective experience. This approach also works in online learning, breaking down the content so there is frequent experimentation, practice, and synthesis.

The Learning Organization engages learners far beyond the classroom: Learning is reinforced in on-site coaching sessions, where both experts and peers engage in reinforcing and applying classroom insights. The "test and experiment" phase of the Kolb's cycle gets extended, leading to new experiences, reflections, and abstractions. This personalized learning is then shared with the greater workplace community through web-based resources, communities of practice, and other settings that maximize its benefits and uncover new possibilities for innovation.

Engaged Pedagogy offers continuous practice and opportunities for learning. Through such approaches, veteran "Wisdom Keepers" within an organization can readily share their knowledge and contribute to the growth and development of the next generation of leadership. Harvesting such wisdom is essential to the innovative organization; help the next generation learn stories from which they can benefit. Making it natural for such sharing to occur paradoxically opens up new innovation channels, for much is gained by experimenting with previous approaches that may still have kernels of benefits.

Exercise: STOP to Appreciate the Moment

WHO: Solo/Group (optional)

WHY: To pause, meditate, and reflect upon the world around you, so you are refreshed and re-energized to be an engaged learner.

HOW:

Step 1 - Take a moment to pause and mindfully appreciate the moment. This prepares us to fully engage in learning using the Kolb cycle. The STOP Practice (adapted here from Russ Harris's work)[27] is an excellent way to do so:

S: Slow down your breathing; or slowly ground yourself, stretch, or press your fingers together.

T: Take note of the world around you with curiosity and appreciation, aware of all you sense (feel, hear, see, smell, taste).

O: Open yourself to make room for thoughts and feelings, allowing them to flow through you fully without judgment.

P: Pursue Values and let them guide you to your next actions.

Then, engage in the following activity:

Step 2 - Settle in a comfortable position. Focus on a single location, object, or thought and look upon it with appreciation and curiosity.

Step 3 - Journal whatever comes to mind, as spontaneously as possible, for 1 minute.

Step 4 - After completing this brief journaling, take another minute or two to reflect upon the things you noticed:

- What did you notice?
- How did it make you feel?
- Why did you notice these things or have these feelings?
- What does it mean if you were to act on any of these insights?

For example: *I am sitting in a room surrounded by photographs from an art exhibit. I focus on one photo, a picture of an open window, with flowers on the sill. I appreciate the beauty of the flowers and think back to when I first visited London as a young man and was struck by so many potted flowers in windows. They are beautiful, and they also absorb CO2, benefiting the environment. Finding beauty in the midst of dirt and urban congestion is one wonderful way people in large cities sustain their humanity and connections to the natural world.*

Step 5 - Take your thinking one step further: Pick any of the suggested actions that emerged from your prior reflection. Create a way of testing or prototyping this new approach.

Taking my previous example: *What if our organization provided cut flowers throughout the building, as well as hanging baskets in public spaces? We could place small vases near copy machines, on cafeteria tables, etc. We could also do more to support the presence of art on stark walls (I've seen this work well). We can create a simple "thank you" fund so staff can award one another flowers for a job well done (this was tried with great success in a school district where I consulted). We can advocate for garden spaces on our grounds that can be tended cooperatively by staff, perhaps in partnership with a school or community group. Etc... etc...*

Step 6 - Finally: Apply your thinking to a real situation or opportunity you are facing. Along with other relevant parties, reflect on the results. In turn, this may lead to other questions worth exploring.

The point of this exercise is to ***experience*** the Kolb Learning Cycle, being actively engaged as a learner. Notice the phases as they played out here: We don't just talk about things, we experience them, then build from that experience so discussions are meaningfully placed in the context of such learning. Whether we take this approach in a classroom, staff meeting, task force, or study group, such an engaged approach to teaching and learning is far more likely to "stick" and be memorable.

LESSON 18: DIVERSITY AND INCLUSION AS CENTRAL TO THE ENTERPRISE

Genuine Inclusion: An Abiding Commitment to Diversity

Many organizations have Diversity Programs that are often well-intentioned but fail to make meaningful differences in the composition of staff or opportunities for all in the workforce. "Diversity Programs" are often simply an invitation to members of underrepresented or marginalized groups to apply for positions, and for members of such groups to conform to the dominant culture should they be hired. Since the basic cultural expectations are not reviewed in a meaningful way, there is relatively little upward movement and the program must continually justify its existence. This dynamic frustrates those from marginalized and underrepresented groups, and tends to make many in privileged positions uncomfortable as efforts fail to result in meaningful change. The pace of change is abysmally slow, data demonstrating benefits can be elusive, and leaders feel constant political pressure to achieve outcomes they may not fully grasp. When change ***does*** occur, some staff now feel they have been unfairly denied certain foregone privileges and replaced by "unqualified" candidates. Hence, resentment grows, even if objective data reflect successes that might be the basis of learning and improvement.

The truly innovative organization culture must include practices that reflect a commitment to genuine inclusion as foundational to other efforts at engagement and diversity. Others have written extensively regarding various approaches to diversity; here are some ideas that align with other practices for What Matters, resulting in a truly inclusive work environment that welcomes cultural diversity in its many forms:

Practice Unwavering Empathy: Create opportunities and norms that reinforce the value of empathy, in relationships among colleagues and between managers and staff. When situations arise where it is difficult for staff to understand one another's experiences, embrace that as a "teachable moment" from which all may grow and improve their sense of community together. This may best be considered in "undiscussables," topics that are often taboo: experiences of race and religious discrimination, harassment, community political issues, etc. These issues can be bridges into deeper understandings of our diverse social experiences and background stories. There is a natural distrust of the Other, and in polarized environments the risks of marginalization for those we consider to be Other can have swift and powerful consequences. There must be a commitment to bridging the cultural divides (both across ethnic cultures and across the subcultures of our organizations): It begins with practicing empathy as leaders and encouraging it throughout the company or agency.[28]

Create Spaces for Difficult Conversations: It is normal in our work lives that there will be turf issues, strained relationships, performance concerns, etc. that require people to engage in difficult, crucial conversations. We need to create specific and predictable spaces that support these discussions in a civil, respectful manner. Such opportunities need to be facilitated in multiple languages, with respectful consideration for the ways Time is framed across cultures, so participants may optimally contribute to policy development, strategic planning, and other conversations that demonstrate meaningful inclusion in the organization's future. The investment of time and resources pays significant dividends in employee retention and engagement, in turn contributing to outstanding customer service.

Use retention, promotion, and productivity metrics to evaluate program success: We need to get way past the idea that "applicant pools" and "hires" sufficiently express our corporate commitment to staff diversity. We need to recognize that diversity and inclusion are complex challenges, where some of the most meaningful outcomes will emerge after considerable time. Rather than using typical "cookie cutter" metrics that typically fill corporate reports and meet short-term political concerns, we must create milestones that align with What Matters and criteria that reflect our Values. These metrics result from ongoing conversations, learning, and program refinements.

View diversity and inclusion as acts of strength and sustenance, rather than as obligations to mitigate risk: Diverse inclusion is not about minority cultures and views accommodating to the entrenched majority and dominant culture; it is about bringing diverse (often divergent) perspectives and experiences to the conversation. Listen carefully and openly to people when they share their experiences of marginalization, fear, and exclusion. Seek out innovative partnerships that welcome new perspectives and experiences, engage all community members and stakeholders in developing potential solutions, and then respectfully assess and evaluate according to the complex issues that are truly presented.

Recognize the company is not an island, but part of a larger social fabric: Pay attention to emerging social issues that influence people's lives: Being a responsible corporate citizen should be intrinsic to the fabric of a company that truly values diversity. Consider the "triple bottom line" of economic, social, and environmental return on investment, for these are more accurate measures of success in this enterprise. **In the end, recognize that all is intertwined here.**[29]

Exercise: Diversity and Inclusion as Central to What Matters at Work

WHO: Solo/Group (optional)

WHY: To better understand and appreciate ways individuals bring unique experiences to their work lives, thus enriching workplace culture.

HOW:

Step 1 - A key Human Resources professional association, CUPA-HR, has been articulating the importance of diversity and inclusion by curating stories of HR professionals in higher education and how they have experienced challenges in this area. Read some of the stories they have collected: www.diversity.cupahr.org

Step 2 - Reflect on the practices identified for valuing diversity and inclusion in the workplace.

- What is your personal story? (You may consider your Core Story from earlier)
- What are your organization's stories? Do we actually know them, understand them, and work together on the basis of shared understandings?
- How well are the personal stories of our members reflected in the practices and priorities of our organization as it does its work?

Step 3 - You might want to use the CUPA-HR stories as a catalyst for community conversations in this area (as we did at UW-Madison in our HR community, which was quite useful). Facilitate at least one such conversation and work with colleagues, to understand those aspects that emerge for further conversation and action. As before, be sure to revisit your own Values and Intentions at this point in the journey.

LESSON 19: RECRUITMENT, RETENTION, AND THE 1ST YEAR EXPERIENCE

"Start at the very beginning. It's a very good place to start." - Maria in The Sound of Music (1965)

Any of us who have had kids can recall what it is like in the first month at a new school. We can probably remember those schools and teachers that did an excellent job facilitating that transition: Creating welcoming places that offer the new student ways to connect with others, they find their way, and know where there are resources that help them flourish. Our children likely wanted to make friends, do well in classes, and "fit in" to the culture and expectations of the school.

New employees undergo similar experiences: While it is exciting to receive that offer and move to a new community or organization, it is also anxiety-producing and overwhelming. There is also immediate pressure to perform, feel successful, and move past feelings of loss you may have about secure relationships left behind from your previous workplace. As with students, there is also a desire to "fit in" and be accepted.

We are past the days where Orientation was a *pro forma* exercise, overwhelmed with useless information – or are we? Many companies and agencies theoretically have "Onboarding" processes to welcome new employees and have them succeed. But beyond making certain our computers work and there is a lunch to meet new colleagues, most organizations throw new employees into the mix of projects and meetings with little attention to the big picture, often confessing that "you'll catch on" as the expectation of the day.

Over the past several years, attention to the "first 90 days" has been expanded to look at the entire "first year experience" as a critical time for employee retention and success. And if we connect this thinking to our other conversations about inclusion and diversity (Lesson 18), as well as attention to Individual Development Plans (Lesson 15), we can readily notice that managers have a special opportunity and responsibility to focus on new employee success from that hiring letter on through the annual review. These ideas further connect to the importance of improving Wellness and Well-Being in our workplaces (Lesson 13), all of which invite an important set of questions:

- As managers and leaders, how do we make our organization one that is truly inviting, so new employees can fully engage and feel welcome?
- What structures already exist to support such efforts? Where are they lacking or absent?
- How do we align our practices in this regard with our Intentions and Values?

Here are some important responses to these questions:

Recruitment and Selection Process: Consider from the start how we represent our organization to those who seek to join it. Of course, recruit diverse applicant pools from an array of sources. But carefully consider who is involved reviewing applications, communicating with candidates, participating in interviews, and ultimately making hiring decisions. Maintain regular communication, so candidates know they have your attention (all too often, applicants do not hear unless they are advanced to the next round, which can take months). And create ways for those involved at various stages of the process to communicate and coordinate with one another, resulting in an integrated selection process that aligns with the needs of the position and its value to the organization.

At each point of contact, genuinely convey to applicants the commitment they should expect from you and your organization should they join you. In the hiring letter, convey What Matters clearly and invite that new employee to immediately consider how they can make a contribution.

Orient with Clear Intention - the First Thirty Days are Critical: "You never get a second chance to make a first impression," right? Plan beyond the "welcome lunch" so the new employee can succeed and not be overwhelmed. Carefully consider that first week and month: How do we help the new person feel welcome and how do we inspire them to be successful? How do we let them know we will keep our promises about opportunities for growth and development?

Utilize peer mentors from both within and outside the hiring department to expand the pool of resources available during this time. Identify critical training to get started (different from other training that may help later) to assure new staff don't stagnate, and create early supervision sessions to clarify where they may need information and where they can flourish on their own. Do you remember Hersey and Blanchard's Situational Leadership Model?[30] It helps clarify what is needed at each phase of employee development, so it can be a guide here, as well.

Establish Goals Through Ongoing Communication: While initial goal-setting is fine in the first month, true performance goals can crystallize after ninety days. These become the basis for ongoing conversations and adjustments between the supervisor and new employee. Rather than thinking about performance reviews (which most research indicates are counter-productive if done as a mere ritual of compliance), engage in meaningful conversations regarding What Matters – look at the first several lessons of this guide to offer examples of worthwhile activities.

Develop an IDP within the first year: We have discussed this tool as a resource for you (Lesson 15), but it is also an excellent resource for you as a supervisor. Introduce the IDP and arrange for your new staff member to receive guidance on how it may best serve their needs. Integrate the results into goal-setting to carry beyond the first year.

Explore Ongoing Mentoring Opportunities: While initial peer mentors may be valuable connections for a new employee, many find support through professional associations and other networks. Encourage development of such connections and look for ways new and veteran staff can connect across organizational divides, such as through communities of practice. Let the staff member be your guide, but always remain vigilant regarding What Matters to the organization and to you.

The above activities should be integrated into a holistic effort to identify, hire, welcome, and sustain the new employee. Consciously evaluate the results of such efforts, so hiring managers learn from experience and improve this aspect of organizational culture over time. All too often, whatever learning happens for an individual manager remains in that person's area of knowledge or a specific department; share experiences (good or bad) across the organization so broader insights and improvements may result.

Exercise: Engage New Staff to Thrive

WHO: Solo/Pair

WHY: To improve our understanding of how we currently engage new staff, then engage in activities to help them thrive in our organization.

HOW:

Step 1 - Many of us are unaware of the resources available to support our efforts to welcome and retain new staff. Here is one place to start: UW-Madison Learning and Talent Development hr.wisc.edu/professional-development/. While many organizations offer professional development opportunities, University of Wisconsin-Madison's Office of Learning and Talent Development has a well-developed set of resources, courses, and specialists that partner with managers and HR professionals to make such connections with new employees so they may succeed and thrive in their work.

Step 2 - Spend some time considering the strategies offered above:

- What is one thing you can do, starting with the next person you hire or otherwise start supervising?
- If you aren't a supervisor, identify a colleague with such responsibility and engage in a conversation that offers these strategies...
- How might you, as a colleague focused on What Matters at Work, support your friend with utilizing such approaches?

Sustain the Journey - Nourish Yourself and Others

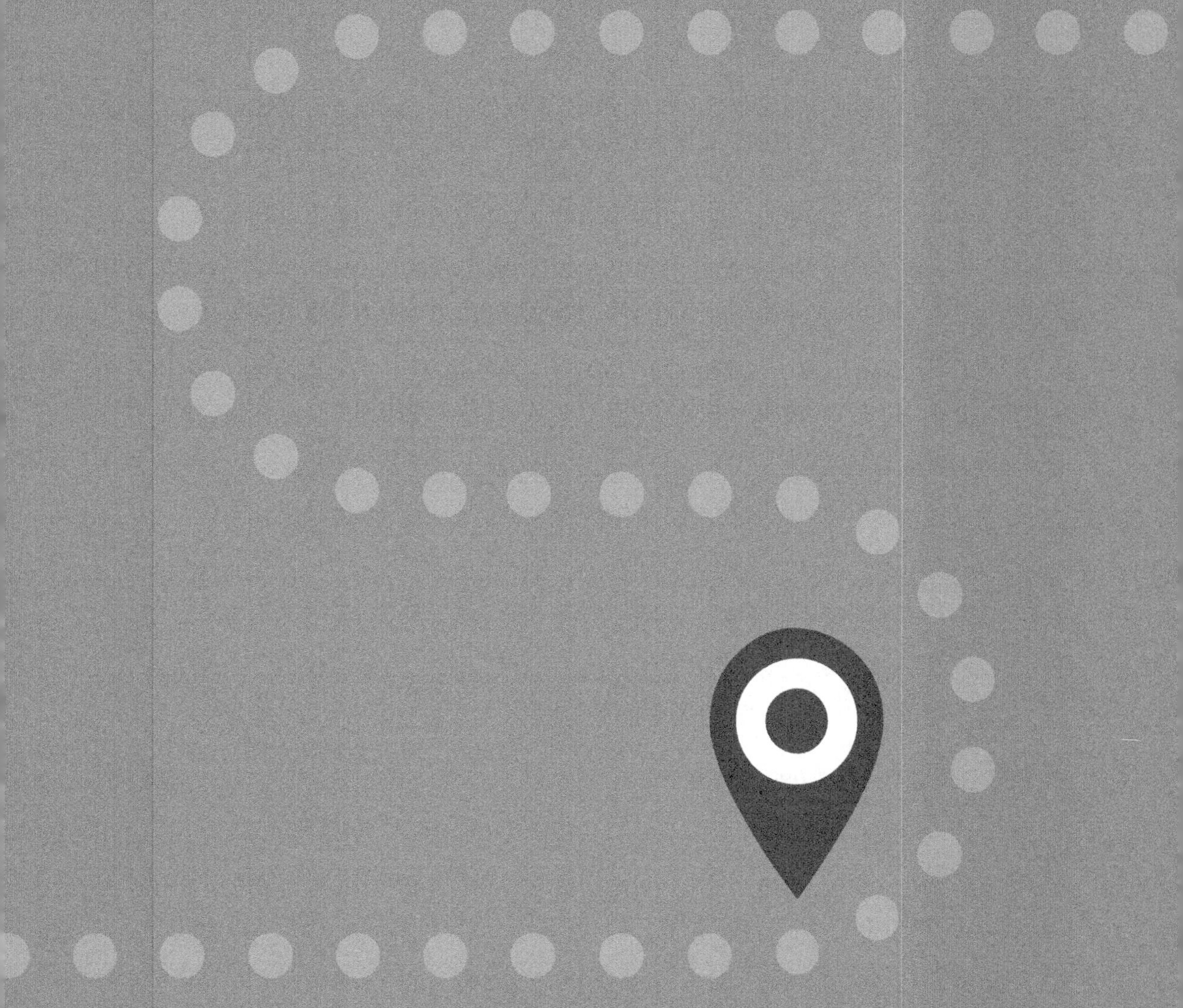

"All of the most important change stories in the world begin with the phrase, "Some friends and I started talking..." - Margaret Wheatley, Turning To One Another (2002)[31]

I genuinely believe that small groups are the building blocks of sustainable change. I also believe that the Relationship is fundamental to the trust, respect, transparency, and vulnerability required to speak honestly and navigate difficult conversations. By developing meaningful, honest relationships at work, we can utilize some powerful tools and processes that help us uncover viable solutions to critical business challenges. While the tools we always seem to crave are useful in themselves, they make little sense and encounter great resistance if we fail to establish a context in which to use them.

These next few lessons share tools and processes that can offer practical ways to successfully take this Journey, being true to ourselves and offering leadership to others so we may sustain one another along the way...

LESSON 20: LEAD FROM EVERYWHERE

A lovely little book, *The Art of Possibility*, by Benjamin Zander and Rosamund Stone Zander (2000) always inspires me. Among the gems included is the idea of "leading from every chair," where Benjamin Zander recounts stories from the youth orchestra he conducted for many years and relates them to his philosophy of leadership. **Consider your position to be one with boundless**

potential to provide leadership in service to the greater aspirations and challenges before your group, wherever you may sit on the hierarchy and perceived power structure.

The practical questions are, *"How do we offer Leadership in a way that is sustainable, healthy for us and nourishing of others, while also expending necessary energy towards the challenge before us?"* And *"How do we lead from everywhere in the organization, regardless of positional power or status?"*

Exercise: Refocusing to Offer Leadership

WHO: Solo/Pair

WHY: Back in Lesson 1, we used a mindful practice to prepare to notice our Intentions for the day. Taking this concept further, the routine practice of centering techniques allows us to return to a place of rest and focus again on those core Intentions whenever they are needed. This activity helps us remain focused on What Matters, to be sure. But it also relieves stress, allows positivity to engage our minds, and physically enables us to access resources in our brains that can ultimately be applied to solving the pressing challenges we face. Finally, it allows us to be prepared to listen empathically and non-judgmentally to those with whom we need to engage, from which we may discover the key ideas and feelings that we must understand and negotiate through our workdays.

HOW:

Step 1 - In his book, *ACT Made Simple* (2009), Russ Harris offers a straight-forward format for constructing mindfulness exercises:

- Notice X.
- Let go of your thoughts.
- Let your feelings be.[32]

Using this approach:

- Take a moment to notice your surroundings.
- Focus on what you are noticing, and let go of other thoughts.
- Feel whatever you are feeling, and be aware of these feelings in the moment.

With practice, this simple exercise can bring you back from distractions, whether they are worries, feelings of apprehension, or feelings of being overwhelmed in the moment. Once achieved, you may return to the task at hand, or otherwise reframe your problem-solving efforts.

Step 2 - In a quiet place (though perhaps with some background sounds to muffle outside noises):

Focus on your Intention. Get grounded physically so you are relaxed and open to sensing what is important to perceive at this time, with distractions reduced as much as possible;

Recall two or three key Values that guide you. As you notice them, remember that you are a capable individual who offers your skills and talents in service to others and consistent with these Values.

Take 2-3 minutes to calmly breathe, relax, and focus in this manner. Then: Notice the question we posed above, "How do we offer Leadership in a way that is sustainable, healthy for us and nourishing of others, while also expending necessary energy towards the challenge before us?" Take several minutes to contemplate this question in an open and non-judgmental manner.

Journal your emerging responses to the question. This may be your conclusion for now, or you may now proceed to the next step.

Step 3 - Meet with a trusted colleague, preferably someone who has already been a partner on this Journey with you before. Discuss what is now emerging for you. Identify specific action steps and resources available for you to offer these responses in a constructive, healthy, and sustainable manner.

••

On a personal level, to "lead from everywhere" has become one of my most important challenges in this work. It has taught me that whenever I feel stuck, overwhelmed, or powerless to create the change I seek in the world, I can rediscover my focus. I am reminded of those things that I am passionate about, reducing the "noise" that distracts me inside my head or the toxic relationships that may undermine my resolve. If I regularly engage in this activity, it becomes so normal to me that I scarcely have to summon any special energy to do it. And because I am engaging in this effort in partnership with others, I find that it not only energizes me, but contagiously engages others to rededicate their efforts to follow their Intentions and Values in service to their Core Story.

Further Wandering: "Pause, Reflect, Transform, Act"

"This space allows for a Pause, that allows Reflection, that leads to Insight, Transformation and, as necessary, to Needed Action."

For many years, I kept these words on an index card on my office desk. They reminded me, as needed, of my Intention and my focus in work. As an educator and facilitator, such words are important: My intention, ever mindful, is to create and cultivate spaces in which people are safe to Pause, Reflect, gain needed Insight, Transform their perspectives on the challenges that face them, and move effectively into Needed Action. This is one key purpose of education, it seems to me. It serves each of us in our efforts to address the meaningful challenges of our lives, which in turn are committed to furthering our sustained presence in service to our loved ones and the Greater Good. Plato made it simple, inviting us to strive for Truth, Beauty, and Good.

As an educator, my role is to support all habits, skills, and knowledge acquisition in service to this basic enterprise. I create spaces in which I help people with their Learning Journey: To help people clarify the specific questions that need to be answered, connect them with resources to seek effective responses, and then find Pathways through which to navigate safely and effectively.

Over time, we help people understand the challenges that are meaningful to them, tease out their assets and gifts to address them, reinforce skills and habits they have already acquired that can be useful, and then offer a worthwhile dose of new skills that add value to their efforts. Then, they are "turned loose" on the world with these new insights, get critical opportunities to practice, test, assess results, practice further, bring new questions, and then integrate new understandings into their actions in relationship to the meaningful challenge.

Of course, since the new insights may conflict with their old paradigm, or be at odds with colleagues or family, the "test period" offers critical opportunities to check our resolve, clarify, persist, be resilient in the face of obstacles, and develop capacity to invent new solutions that are adaptable and sustainable. Rarely does the first attempt "solve the problem," for the challenges being faced are complex and often long-standing. As such, our Newtonian preference for simple, mechanical explanations gives way to Quantum uncertainties, ambiguities, and (at times) disillusionment. It's a tough path: trail blazing is fraught with danger and filled with fear and anxiety.

If we keep in mind the simplicity of the practice, we can harness its wisdom for increasingly complex challenges. Pause... Reflect... Transform through Insight... Take Appropriate Action.

LESSON 21: COLLABORATIVE NEGOTIATION

We define collaboration here as "working together to achieve a common goal or purpose." Notice that collaboration is much more than simply "working together." It is to do so "to achieve a common goal or purpose." ***It is a process that engages participants in a genuine exploration of their common needs and interests, through which they seek mutually beneficial outcomes.*** It can be easily contrasted with coordination (where we communicate from our separate positions and needs, but try not to step on each other's toes) and cooperation (where we seek to achieve our independent interests, rather than focus on those that are shared). Collaboration has the potential to invent new identities and ways of relating to one another, ways of forging a sense of "We" beyond "You" and "I" in our work together.

Collaboration is a "Best Practice" to be learned, practiced, modeled, and developed throughout the organization. How do we do this? In Collaborative Negotiation (also known as "Interest-based Negotiation" and "Principled Negotiation"), the parties involved seek to understand one another's concerns and find solutions that both address independent interests and those that are shared. It transcends compromise, which merely seeks a midpoint between negotiating positions. This approach seeks to reach agreements that address both the substantive issues that bog us down at work and to promote more sustainable relationships that can be called upon to address other issues in the future.

Six Stage Collaborative Negotiation Process[33]

Stage 1: Assess personal/group needs, desired outcomes

Consider the burning questions you bring to the situation: "What Matters to me? What do I believe Matters to the group? What do we each seek as desired outcomes or results of our work together?" Substantive, Procedural, and Relational needs are all worthy of consideration. Substantive needs refer to the "stuff" being negotiated, such as program priorities, budget allocations, or staff roles. Procedural needs refer to the process by which we address the "stuff": Is the process perceived to be fair, inclusive, with decision-making made in a broadly understood manner? Finally, Relational needs express concerns regarding trust, respect, honesty, safety, and similar issues that arise in relationships while negotiating the substance of our work together.

Take some time to clarify these responses before proceeding to a conversation with others. If you are facilitating such a process, be sure to clarify responses from each person participating in the conversation.

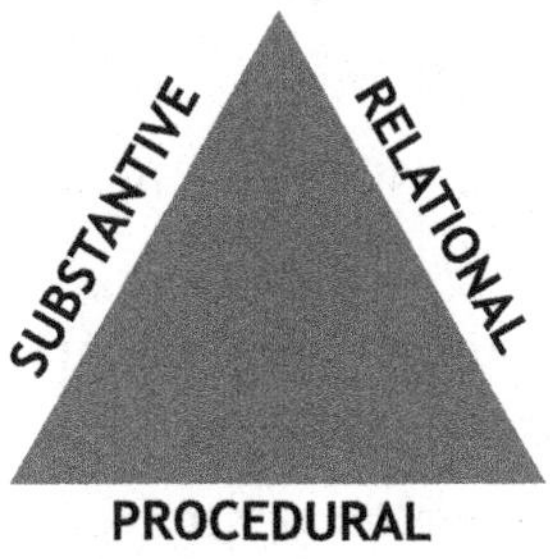

Needs in Negotiation

Stage 2: Establish Ground Rules

In beginning the conversation, go through the ritual of establishing our expectations regarding how we might have a safe and constructive environment in which to discuss difficult, perhaps conflictive, issues. This ritual is important as a point of reference for maintaining such a space.

Stage 3: Identify Initial Positions

Honestly discuss what you want from one another. Work hard to listen to one another, demonstrating a commitment to understand each other's needs, interests, and concerns. People may enter the conversation with specific ideas regarding solutions - allow those to be surfaced as a starting point that is honest, even if it appears to be problematic as diametrically opposed positions are expressed.

Stage 4: Explore Underlying Interests/Concerns/Needs

Try to understand –together –the deeper "Why" at the heart of the conversation: "What are the interests, concerns, and needs that represent the Values and Intentions at the heart of the inquiry? How do these reflect issues that lie beneath the surface?" Patiently navigate this phase of the conversation, seeking to fully understand one another before proceeding towards solutions.

Stage 5: Develop Mutually Satisfying Solutions

(Both process and solutions). Take time to review emerging Agreements, both in terms of the solutions and the process by which the group negotiated them.

- Taking one issue at a time;
- Generate several possible responses to the concerns that have been expressed;
- Defer judgment and clarify criteria by which eventual solutions might be assessed;
- As appropriate, develop prototype solutions that can be tested;
- Seek mutually acceptable criteria; and
- Build agreements by a consensus of those engaged.

Stage 6: Evaluate Outcomes (Both Process and Solutions)

Take time to review emerging Agreements, both in terms of the solutions and the process by which the group negotiated them. Use "Hallmarks of a Good Agreement" to evaluate how well the Agreements serve you:

- **Fairness** in the eyes of those who negotiated them
- **Balance,** meaning all have a stake in implementation
- **Realism,** so the parties involved actually have the capacity to implement actions

- **Specificity**, clear enough to be actionable
- **Self-enforcement**, as much as possible, by those at the table
- **Being Future-oriented**, considering how we might address such issues as the naturally occur again

It is often beneficial to test Agreements for a few days or weeks and then check back together to see how they are working or could be improved.

Exercise: Collaborative Negotiation Application

WHO: Group

WHY: To practice the above process, utilizing realistic workplace scenarios.

HOW:

Step 1 - Using one of the Scenarios provided in Appendix A, follow the Six-Step Process.

Step 2 - Debrief with fellow participants:

- What worked well? What challenges did you encounter and how did you address them?
- How does this process compare to the usual practice in your organization?
- How might you practice further and bring this approach to real conversations that need to occur?

Step 3 - Journal your resulting insights... look for opportunities to apply what has been learned in your daily work.

LESSON 22: DIFFICULT CONVERSATIONS THAT MATTER

People generally want to get along together. Indeed, most of us tend to avoid tensions and conflicts as much as possible, all in the name of workplace harmony. However, there are diverse (sometimes conflicting) perspectives on how best to accomplish our work. There are also varying sources of power and privilege throughout the organization, and these impact how well these perspectives are expressed and accepted into organizational cultures. Yet if we are truly committed to our organization thriving, we need to engage directly and honestly in conversations that matter.

Here is a simple format that can bring us back "on track" when we feel things are slipping away. It combines approaches from three sources: *Having Difficult Conversations* (Stone, Patton, and Heen, 2010), *Crucial Conversations* (Patterson et al, 2002), and *The Art of Focused Conversation* (Stanfield, Ed., 2000), as well as insights gleaned from many experiences with work groups.

The Three Conversations

There are actually three conversations taking place:

The ***substantive conversation*** is about the "stuff," the project at hand (for example). Often, this frames our initial sense of the Agenda for a meeting, but it is too narrowly focused to embrace all that is really going on here. If there was a catalyzing event, this is often a starting point for "What happened?"

The ***emotional conversation*** is about how we discuss the emotional aspects: Is there a sense that we can honestly discuss our feelings together? Is there a perception that we have "hidden agendas" or other expectations that make it feel less likely we can openly discuss the project?

Finally, the ***identity conversation*** is about the safety of engaging in the process to discuss the substance: I ask myself, *"Does it feel* *"safe," or am I concerned for my reputation, job, or other things I hold near and dear to me?"* A person's identity feeling threatened can be an extremely powerful factor in a difficult conversation.

All difficult conversations contain within them these three conversations: If we are to get at the deeper meaningful issues at hand, all three must be respected. Furthermore, as a "high stakes" conversation, we should anticipate divergent perspectives, meanings, and beliefs about what is possible to address the deeper concerns here. As noted in the lesson on Collaborative Negotiation, we want to focus on those underlying needs, interests, and concerns when seeking solutions and developing agreements together. This process helps us enter that world, perhaps at a point where there are two or three project team members seeking to "clear the air" after a frustrating exchange.

ORID - Using Focused Conversation Method

Finally, keep in mind four levels of inquiry - known as ORID or "Focused Conversation Method"[34] – that can anchor your openness in seeking to understand one another:

- What are some objective data that you notice in order to address the situation? (Objective)
- How do you (and others) feel about what you are hearing from one another? (Reflective)
- What is meaningful to you as you review this information and express these feelings? (Interpretive)
- Now... what are you going to do? (Decisional)

All too often, we simply move to the "action" or "decision" question in our meetings, especially in difficult conversations that make us uncomfortable. By utilizing the Objective, Reflective, Interpretive, and Decisional levels of inquiry, we can better discipline ourselves to uncover those things we are noticing, our blind spots, and our experiences that occur as a result of such learning together. Only when we understand these answers is the question, "What are we going to do?" ripe for investigation.

Exercise: Difficult Conversations Using ORID

WHO: Solo/Pair

WHY: To apply Focused Conversation Method (ORID) to a "difficult conversation" that needs to occur.

HOW: (Use *Difficult Conversation Worksheet*, in Appendix B)

Step 1 – Clarify for yourself:

- How do you define this conversation? What are your frames for the substantive, emotional, and identity conversations contained within it?
- What specific changes do you seek as a result of this conversation? Is it clear why these changes matter to you?
- What would you like the other person to understand as a result of this conversation?
- How will you know the changes that result will have addressed your needs in the substantive, emotional, and identity conversations?

Step 2 – Answer the above questions, then find a partner or colleague with whom to practice this conversation. Help your partner understand the likely answers to these questions from the perspective of the real person you are imagining here. Follow the ORID levels of inquiry to keep the conversation focused. As appropriate, after practicing, have a genuine meaningful conversation with the other person(s) involved in the situation.

Step 3 – After practicing (or after a real conversation), reflect:

- How well did the conversation align with my expectations?
- To what degree my desired results achieved?
- What supported or undermined our ability to achieve the desired results?
- How did my behavior contribute to the success of the conversation?
- How did it inhibit such efforts?

A simplified version of this ORID approach can be found in *Liberating Structures* (Lipmanowicz and McCandless, 2014), where they have devised, *"What? So What? Now, What?"* as questions to similarly guide inquiry and decisions. In either approach, the discipline of patiently navigating these levels of inquiry results in the types of thoughtful discussions that are required for effective consensus to be reached. With practice, staff can readily integrate this approach and apply it to an array of discussions. As we get better at the process, we can readily call upon it for those decisions that require true and meaningful consensus.

LESSON 23: NAVIGATE CONFLICT IN THE WORKPLACE

Conflicts in many organizations cannot be discussed or addressed. They are, as Ryan and Ostreich described it over twenty years ago, "undiscussables" (*Driving Fear out of the Workplace*, 1998). In my nearly forty years as a mediator focusing on workplace and organizational disputes, I have found that little has changed: Many organizations tolerate high levels of toxic, dysfunctional conflict and then create convenient narratives that explain employee departures ("she wanted a new experience"), reorganization ("they needed a shakeup to avoid getting stale"), or even the reassignments of leaders ("it's normal to change leadership every few years"). They never address underlying systemic or interpersonal issues that have made organizations places of perpetual fear, backbiting, gossip, and turf protection.

Conflicts arise when the parties involved perceive a threat to their needs, interests, or concerns. People respond to the perceived threat, whether intended by the other parties or not. They frame these perceptions through "perceptual filters" and cultural narratives; my gender, race, religion, language, and other identity frames are critical to this understanding. As such, we may have vastly different things we notice in the situation, and distinct ideas about what might be acceptable solutions that address the threat posed by the conflict.

What is threatened? In most workplaces, we are likely focused on power, roles, reputation, and areas of responsibility. People perceive that such things – which may relate to their Core Stories – may be lost if not protected. These situations often go unaddressed for many months or years, so the organization loses a great deal of productivity from key staff who resign, refuse to work with one another, or simply withdraw their energies.

We are building here on what has been discussed in this Section: These are difficult conversations (see Lesson 22), and they often require collaborative negotiation to address (see Lesson 21). What is added here are specific steps to address the underlying threats to our needs, interests, and concerns that are both sources of fear and keys to transformative learning. Indeed, addressing workplace conflict is a critical element of What Matters.

Follow this three-phase process:

Phase 1: Prepare

Focus and prepare for the conversation. Engage in focused breathing and other centering practices. Notice your thoughts and feelings: *What are your underlying needs, interests, and concerns? How are they threatened by the conflict?*

Identify your desired outcomes or results from this conversation. (You may have several, so focus on 2-3 key outcomes for now) *What is likely to occur if you cannot work it out together?* (This is important to understand, especially if you feel like abandoning the discussion)

Consider "Ground Rules" needed for a safe and constructive conversation. *"What rules do I need to have this conversation?"*

Phase 2: Understand the Issues

Establish Ground Rules together, so that they are mutually acceptable. Common examples may include one person speaking at a time, listening fully to one another, and understandings of confidentiality. This is the first agreement.

Express concerns to one another. Listen fully to the other person, without interruption. As helpful, restate what you each understand to be the other person's perspective. Be open to discovering a different story than the one you've assumed to be true.

Phase 3: Work It Out

Identify the issues to be addressed, and agree on a scope and order to this conversation... there may be a need for further research, involving others, or additional discussions.

Discuss one issue at a time, generating options or possible solutions without judgment or quick decisions. Clarify criteria (Why does this idea work? Why doesn't it?). As appropriate, take note of areas of agreement. As well, identify issues that may require further discussion or information before any solutions can be identified - you may even agree to prototype certain promising ideas.

Build a meaningful agreement (note the earlier "Hallmarks of a Good Agreement") and agree to "check in" together in the coming days. Try not to allow issues to fester or unanticipated obstacles to become new sources of blame.

This process can be adapted to third party roles, where you facilitate or mediate a dispute involving others: Indeed, we will offer you this challenge. It has additional levels of complexity in group disputes (which may involved multiple parties, not only more people), but the same general format serves us well.[35]

There are two major adaptations with groups:

- Think carefully about time and be sure to allow for longer discussion as group size increases. We are often surprised at how quickly time passes in such conversations.
- Individual motivations and levels of entrenchment will vary. We tend to hear from "extremists" in groups, as they feel strongly and have much to say about the issues. We also need to hear, however, from "moderates;" while they

may tend to defer to others, they can often see "both sides" and thus may offer reasonable pathways to successful agreements.

Exercise: Conflict Resolution Application

WHO: Pair

WHY: To practice a process for addressing workplace conflicts successfully.

HOW:

Step 1 - Using one of the Scenarios provided in Appendix A, follow the Process outlined above. Debrief with fellow participants:

- What worked well? What challenges did you encounter and how did you address them?
- How does this process compare to usual practice in your organization?
- How might you practice further and bring this approach to real conversations that need to occur?

Step 2 - Journal your resulting insights... look for opportunities to apply what has been learned in your daily work.

LESSON 24: INTEGRATE DISPUTE SETTLEMENT SYSTEMS

Note: There are three exercises associated with this Lesson, each building upon the previous one. Time commitment is ongoing for the emerging Work Group, so take this into account in approaching the activities.

Conflicts and complaints naturally arise within most organizations. Although they offer profound learning and growth opportunities, they are painful. We tend to respond, therefore, by either channeling such issues to formal grievance processes or by ignoring them as much as possible until they are too big to manage effectively. One of the difficulties with formal responses is that they tend to focus on people's *rights and legal protections*, rather than the true *needs and interests* of the people involved. As Fisher and Ury (*Getting to Yes*, originally in 1983, revised in 2011) pointed out long ago, this is the opposite of what is required; we need to cultivate dispute settlement systems that facilitate the honest expression of the core concerns people face, from which durable, meaningful solutions can be achieved.

We need to do better: We need approaches that can result in holistic, meaningful responses and longer-term solutions to workplace disputes. These are essential to organizational health and for bringing forth new ideas that benefit our work together and challenge the status quo, managing conflicts that naturally arise. In turn, new approaches help raise important questions about reforms and hold all members of the community accountable to its Core Values.

Three types of dispute settlement systems facilitate constructive approaches to conflict:

Informal Systems

All organizations have those "go to" people that everybody relies upon to listen well, offer solid advice, and otherwise be a presence in solving problems and settling disputes. This practice builds upon this naturally occurring phenomenon.

Exercise: Identifying Informal Dispute Settlement Resources

WHO: Work Team

WHY: To understand and "map" the informal resources that currently exist to manage disputes in your organization, then to consider how to better align these approaches with What Matters.

HOW:

Step 1 - Survey staff to identify overall perspectives on conflicts in the workplace and how empowered they feel they are to address them. Such a survey can be connected to a broader climate survey or employee engagement effort, for it helps us understand training needs that we can act upon to address priority concerns.

Step 2 - But let's add one more question: "Please identify up to 5 people in the organization you believe are especially skilled as listeners and as people who help solve conflicts as they arise."

Step 3 - Once collected, use these results to invite members of this nominated group to a meeting in which they can be recognized and thanked for their natural contributions, and from which they can be asked to offer suggested ways we can improve the company's ability to foster communication, collaboration, and conflict resolution efforts. Then be prepared to follow through on those suggestions that have resonance with organizational Core Values.

Non-Formal Systems

This is a term that may be new to many readers: "Non-formal" systems are intentionally organized approaches that largely depend upon peer leadership and agenda-setting. They can be contrasted to the informal systems that simply arise and end naturally, or the formal systems that tend to be integrated with policy, governance, and top-down leadership. Non-formal practices include communities of practice and similar learning communities. In dispute resolution, they include Peer Facilitation and Peer Mediation projects. In these systems, a cross-section of staff across the organization is trained to mediate staff disputes, and is promoted as being available for such efforts. While the project can be connected to HR or other management, its reputation and success depends upon the abilities of peer facilitators to be perceived as impartial sources of service, and that any negotiation among disputing parties is voluntary and self-determined. Peer facilitators can be available to mediate conflicts, facilitate complex problem solving sessions around difficult issues, or to serve as peer listeners and coaches for individuals who want to sort out concerns before engaging in other efforts to address them.

Exercise: Developing Non-Formal Dispute Settlement Systems

WHO: Solo/Work Team

WHY: To build intentional, peer-led approaches for constructively managing conflict in the organization, starting from informal practitioners and resources.

HOW: Go back to that list of people identified in the previous survey. Invite them to discuss the possibility and viability of such a non-formal peer facilitator program:

- Who might they recommend for a cohort of facilitators from which to start?
- What do they recommend regarding how to get broad support from management and staff to pilot such an effort?

This group is an excellent resource, and a bridge to shared ownership of such an initiative.

Formal Systems

Grievance and appeals policies, as well as other channels for formally addressing concerns, are essential to organizational governance. Boards of Directors should establish standing committees in cooperation with both management and staff leadership, so rights are understood and protected and needs are addressed in effective and relatively cost-efficient ways. All involved (whether Staff or Volunteers) in hearing such concerns should be trained to do so, and there should be external resources that add another level of professional skill and review to such processes. This level of investment and oversight is fundamental to the democratically managed organization. From such a vantage point, systematic understandings of the corporate culture can be acted upon; for example, if we find a particular division or service area more commonly has issues that escalate to formal grievance processes, we can investigate the underlying contributing factors and see if there can be systemic solutions that can prevent such conflicts from developing into formal grievances.

At a more detailed level, some organizations have created numerous "governance circles" that follow the rules of highly inclusive processes, such as Holacracy or Sociocracy. As shared earlier, the largest company taking this approach is Zappos, where it is now embedded in the corporate culture. Other examples are described by Frederic Laloux, *Reinventing Organizations* (2014). As noted previously (Lesson 12), Laloux offers examples of "Next-Stage" companies; one of their salient features is the ability to address conflict constructively, inclusively, and in a manner that is respected across the organization. This is hard work, but if we are focused on What Matters, this is essential work that pays huge dividends in employee engagement, retention, and productivity. When combined with First Year efforts (Lesson 19), such approaches to dispute resolution send powerful messages to staff that they are valued and important. As in many examples offered in this Guide, there may be an investment in What Matters that pays dividends through its ultimate productivity, staff retention, and workplace climate improvements.

Exercise: Mapping All Dispute Settlement Systems

WHO: Work Team

WHY: To create a more complete map of ways conflicts are addressed at the current time, so there may be a thorough analysis of formal, informal, and non-formal resources that may be brought to bear on such issues. By understanding "current state," we may realistically start conversations regarding a preferred "future state" for the organization.

HOW:

Step 1 - With others from your organization, create a Mind Map of your company's various places and spaces where disputes are addressed. Be sure to list formal, non-formal, and informal processes as fully as possible:

- What are the actual activities that are occurring? How do they relate to one another?
- Is it clear to staff and customers what these various approaches to conflict are, and how they are accessed?
- Where are your own "blind spots" here, where your map really reflects "uncharted territory" that still needs to be explored?

Step 2 - Have fun... create a "key" that helps tell the story of your various dispute settlement systems. Then consider how best to continue the conversation so improvements can be considered.

Step 3 - Use this initial Mind Map as a point of departure. As conversations continue over time, return to it and create updated versions that reflect the evolution of efforts in this area.

LESSON 25: ENGAGE GROUPS USING BLOCK'S "SIX CONVERSATIONS"

Over many years, Peter Block has offered us numerous tools, stories, and pathways to discover What Matters at Work. Among his books is one especially useful at this juncture in our learning Community: *The Structure of Belonging* (2009, revised 2018) offers personal insights from Block's experiences in Cincinnati, as well as a conceptual model that helps us understand crucial distinctions in approaches to groups and community-building. Earlier, we quoted Block's ideas regarding the role of physical space in building community (Lesson 11). For now, I offer the "Six Conversations" that Block identifies for groups to explore if they seek meaningful change in their organizations or communities:

Invitation

This is the First Conversation. Invitation is required to capture potential participants' attention in the midst of busy, distracted lives, the "subject line" that engages our interest. It is the foundation of hospitality from which other conversations are possible.

Possibility

This is an aspirational conversation, one that challenges us to engage our imaginations to contemplate the unreachable. For example, *"If we were to build an organization that fully expresses our values, what would that look like, sound like, feel like?"*

Ownership

This is a conversation about personal accountability and "skin in the game." *"What are you prepared to contribute in order to fulfill our Possibility?"*

Dissent

Building community requires more than being nice with one another. It involves speaking truthfully and hearing honest areas of difference and dissent. This conversation embraces dissent as an essential stepping stone in that process. *"What are areas of concern and disagreement? What might be alternative approaches that have not been fully considered?"*

Commitment

This conversation asks us how we wish to translate our Ownership into action... *"What are you prepared to do in order to demonstrate your commitment to the project? How are you prepared to respond to obstacles and challenges along the way that sap your energy and question your resolve?"*

Gifts

This is a conversation in which we take stock of our assets, acknowledge what we bring individually and collectively to the enterprise, and consider any "strings" that may be attached to engaging any of those assets. It also helps us notice gaps or areas where other gifts may be required. *"What gifts, strengths, talents, or assets do we each bring to this effort? Collectively, what does this say about our capacity to achieve our Possibility?"*

In practice, each of these conversations can be sequenced in order to facilitate an effective result. For example, if I have a troubled group that has lost energy and momentum, I may follow this approach:

- Offer a compelling Invitation that names the importance of the issue and invites everyone to discuss it openly and honestly.
- Facilitate an Ownership conversation that explores what levels of energy and commitment truly exist, without judgment, for continuing to engage in the work of the group.
- The group should take stock of its assets and Gifts, so we could appreciate the capacities of its members. From there, we could...
- Examine the Possibility and promise offered by this group, transcending the energy-draining nature of the current state of the group.

- I'd also want to be sure Dissenting opinions were explored and respected, before seeking a Commitment regarding future actions.

This sequence makes sense to me in light of my own experience with such groups... you might find another pathway nourishes the conversation and helps the group determine its future.[36]

Several years ago, I convened a ten-week study group that sprang from this excellent text - that could be a great bonus activity for this lesson!

Exercise: Six Conversations

WHO: Group

WHY: To explore the potential value of the various types of conversations described, and how each is a valuable approach in learning What Matters.

HOW:

Step 1 - Bring these questions to a meeting of a group in which you are exploring meaningful change to a project, considering a proposed innovation, or addressing a community matter.

Step 2 - Offer these questions as a way to structure the group's inquiry; engage in whichever of the "Six Conversations" appear to be relevant to the group at this time.

Step 3 - After the meeting:

- What did you notice about these questions?
- How did each make a unique contribution to the discussion?
- As a result, how would you now describe the group in terms of its efforts to get to What Matters in their context?

An additional note in closing: Block argues, in much the same way as the Wandering essay on the next pages, that the small group is the transformative unit of change in society. Rather than feeling overwhelmed by getting large numbers of people involved in a *movement*, Block reminds us that we must begin with a small number engaged in a *moment*; their relationships with one another are the foundation for further efforts.

LESSON 26: CATALYZE CREATIVE PROBLEM-SOLVING IN GROUPS

Another way to foster effective work teams is to facilitate problem solving processes that are genuinely collaborative in nature. When we engage in a shared approach to problem solving that is both creative and collaborative, we invite participation in a way that allows people to leave their titles at the door and welcome ideas from all participants.

UW-MANIAC
(A Success Story)

One exciting way to promote an innovative culture is through dedicated learning about creative approaches to innovation and problem-solving. For many years, I convened a community of practice called "UW–MANIAC" (Madison Area Network for Innovation and Collaboration), through which dozens of educational workshops and conferences cultivated such a culture. The learning community emerged from a unique conference, "Inspiration from Unusual Sources," in 2007.[40] Over the following decade, UW–MANIAC innovated several unique approaches to such learning that resulted in new ways of problem-solving across the organization.[41] In addition,

A Final Wandering: "In the Beginning was the Relationship"

Among the key insights gleaned from our work through the years is that none of us exists in isolation from others, and that the fundamental building block of the universe is the Relationship. Contrary to dominant socialization that focuses so strongly on individualism, we have come to appreciate that Relationships are key to fostering our individual success. When those relationships do not exist or are weakened, the state of mind, energy, and ultimate problem-solving capacities of individuals are often strongly compromised.

This is important, with consequences on how we educate people, how we organize our work places, and how we monitor and respond to issues and concerns that arise in various contexts. We tend to invest in individual training and professional development, and we reward individual accomplishment or criticize individual failure. We give lip-service to "teams" in our classrooms and our workplaces, yet we evaluate performance on such an individualistic basis that such team opportunities are often compromised in terms of their perceived value.

Instead, all individuals need to be understood in terms of their relationships and the contexts in which they exist. If we focus on conditions in which group members can identify and develop their strengths, communicate effectively with one another, develop shared goals and purpose, and ultimately foster interdependent relationships that can sustain collaboration, opportunities for what Warren Bennis calls "great groups" are much more likely to emerge.[37] As noted elsewhere, the "wicked" problems we need to address require a level of nimble flexibility and focus that earlier generations may not have required to such a degree.

How do we foster this capacity, especially in situations requiring innovative responses? Brian Arthur's research on innovative technologies[38] offers a clear path: Facilitate deep development and competence around strength-based domains in individuals and teams, then bring people together within spaces that encourage members to "lower boundaries" across their expertise domains. In such environments, they can be freed to inquire of one another, experiment, prototype possible solutions, and otherwise engage in the stages of the innovation process likely to produce worthy results. Some responses may be incremental, others more radical, but the sheer quantity and quality are likely to be more effective than our typical approaches.

This is also reflected in the work of Nathan Myhrvold, who has parlayed his Microsoft fortune into an array of creative projects, most notably his controversial Intellectual Ventures company. Among his discoveries has been a facilitated process whereby Nobel laureates and others have come together for conversations about whatever they are noticing in the world. Intentionally bringing together diverse experts, Myhrvold has been able to glean hundreds of patent-worthy ideas.[39]

I have experimented with this process in two distinct ways: I have adapted Myhrvold's process to facilitate conversations among scientists in the "Chaos and Complexity Seminar" at the University of Wisconsin-Madison, with fascinating results. These discussions produced excellent ideas regarding salient challenges facing the University, and did so in minimal amounts of time. I also co-created a unique conference format, the "Big Learning Event," that twice brought together innovators and thought leaders from diverse fields of inquiry to foster such interactions and discoveries. When their conversations were offered in the presence of several hundred others who were prepared to observe and then build from what they witnessed, the results were transformative. Indeed, the BLE inspired concrete innovations at the University and was replicated elsewhere.

It doesn't always work, but it seems that this approach reliably fosters more connections, insights, and possibilities than our typical academic and corporate silos. Incorporating such thinking into our organizational dynamics and reinforcing opportunities in the ways we train and evaluate performance can be a highly important way to build Relationship.

UW–MANIAC curated a simple library that became a continuing resource for its members, so they could access tools as needed.[42] The relationships that formed as a result of such learning became powerful resources in addressing critical programmatic, policy, and budget issues, helping align organizational direction with the capacities and priorities of its staff.

Creative Problem Solving in Groups

We are often asking staff teams to think "out of the box" and to bring creativity to their efforts. Yet they often retain boundaries of practicality and past practice, or a lack of resolve to look at issues from a totally new perspective. Therefore, we need to create approaches that encourage such thinking and provide practice around scenarios that stretch people to consider the future in new ways. One classic method is an adaptation of Osborn and Parnes Creative Problem Solving process,[43] an approach that has been taught and used throughout the world. At the heart of such a process are the following steps:

(Form small groups of 4-6 people per group. Select a table facilitator and, as needed, a recorder for each phase.)

Step 1: Generate Ideas

Working from an initial framing of the question (we will revisit this assumption in "Mess Finding" below), your first task is to generate at least 30 possible responses/solutions to the problem in 15 minutes. See the table on the next page, which summarizes several idea generation methods. Start with "silent brainstorming," then shift to another approach or two. Record these ideas in a way that allows you to easily read and evaluate them at a later time.

Step 2: Group Ideas

Grouping is different from ranking or evaluating... just find commonalities among batches of ideas using an agreed upon method.[44] After 15 minutes, you should have several such groupings for your ideas.

Step 3: Rate Ideas

Which ones are worth pursuing further? Using an agreed upon rating/ranking method, group members should identify the "top ideas" that seem to be emerging here... why are they good ideas? Be sure you have identified criteria that you can later understand in making your final decisions.

Step 4: Choose Best Solutions

What decision-making method makes sense in this case? Refer to the Decision Making Matrix we introduced previously (see Lesson 8). Discuss which approach makes sense in this case, given the expertise and authority of this group. Then use an agreed upon approach to make a decision. Articulate the group's solution, so it may be clearly understood by those receiving it.

"Mess Finding" (Possible Pre-Work)

Let's return to the issue of "Mess Finding": Sometimes, the presenting formulation of a problem actually misses the point. It frames the presenting symptoms and overlooks the underlying issue. As such, it can be helpful to first do some "Mess Finding" before engaging in the above process. This pre-work asks the question, *"What might be some underlying problems to be found within the presenting problem?"*

Brainstorm up to 10 possible underlying problems, looking at the issue from a variety of perspectives. Then frame a new problem, using the format:

"How might we (strong action verb) (object) so that (a meaningful goal) might result in (context)?" Offer an example, related to the presenting issue we've been using to illustrate the process. Once so framed, we engage in the four-step process outlined earlier.

STRATEGY	PROCESS
Silent Brainstorming	Quietly write down as many ideas as you can, without judgment or analysis.
Imagine a Famous Person	What would they say?
Piggy Back	"Yes, I like that idea because_____________, AND..."
Associate Ideas	Look at a poster, pictures, objects, statements (phrases) and use them as a primer or jumping off point for a new idea.
Integrate Multiple Ideas	(Famous person, object association– e.g. "What would Rachel Carson do if she were living today in California, facing intense wildfires?")
Unreality	What ideas do you have that are WAY out there?
Bothers	Find things that bother you about the subject and turn them into positive ideas.
Nominal Group Process	Individual silent brainstorming followed by round robin idea sharing and grouping.

Brainstorming and Other Idea Generation Strategies

Exercise: Creative Problem-Solving

WHO: Group

WHY: To engage in a collaborative approach to problem-solving that also sparks creativity and new insights gained from how issues are framed.

HOW:

Step 1 - Follow the steps outlined above, using one of the Scenarios we have developed. (See Appendix A)

Step 2 - Then debrief with participants:

- What are some strengths of this approach that could be useful to our organization and context?
- What might be challenging to apply and adapt?
- What else do we need to learn in order to best apply this approach?

LESSON 27: AN ENLIGHTENED APPROACH TO ASSESSMENT

When addressing challenges we face, we need to distinguish among the types of problems being addressed. Michael Quinn Patton (*Developmental Evaluation*, 2010, and other writings) has created an excellent taxonomy of issues that serves us here:

Simple Problems

Some issues can be addressed by a recipe that can be easily replicated. There is high reliability that if you follow the recipe, you will achieve the same result each time. Examples of simple problems are fast food recipes (you expect a Big Mac, for example, to be prepared in the same way with the same result at any McDonald's franchise in the world), warehouse storage strategies, usual payroll practices, room setup processes, and many maintenance problems. In order to solve a Simple problem reliably, you train towards sameness: if we teach employees how to serve food on the lunch line, for example, they can repeat that skill in settings and deliver predictable results. Simple problems are often accompanied by "best practices," tried and true approaches that are readily shared and available across the organization and, in many cases, across the industry (see ISO 9000 standards, for example).

Complicated Problems

There are other issues that are characterized by a larger number of variables, which sometimes can be disaggregated to become a chain of simple problems. A large mathematical formula is such a complicated problem, and by following the order of operations, you can solve it. Sending a spaceship to the moon is solved this way, following the laws of math and physics, with 99.99% reliability. But there is another important element of most complicated problems: There are several ways to go about solving them, resulting in natural social and technical tensions among members of a problem solving team. Some prefer to work more independently, while others like to communicate regularly.

Some are deductive, others are inductive. Some can call upon past experiences from similar problems, while others can draw upon vastly different experiences. These tensions often result in conflicts over how best to solve the problem, especially as members get entrenched in their own preferred approaches and communication breaks down. There are truly several "better practices" in most Complicated problems, and each practice has its unique social and technical benefits and costs. Much of the work in scientific laboratory research, surgical team procedures, strategic planning processes, and menu planning for catering operations all are truly Complicated problems.

Complex Problems

Finally, there are complex problems (sometimes called, "Wicked problems"), and they are characterized by uncertainty, dynamism, and powers of emergence. They lack the predictability of either Simple or Complicated problems, and often exhibit disproportionate impacts of variables as a result. While large amounts of data can be helpful, it is still a quality of Complexity that there will be significant uncertainty. In life, examples abound: raising a child, experiencing romance, reacting to surprise. There is little predictability involved in assessing strategies and responses to such problems. In the workplace, many of the issues we have been discussing are Complex problems: relationships among work teams, strategic planning in the midst of vast change, reinventing an established organization or starting one in a totally new market space. Complex problems are not approached by just throwing up our hands and praying for insight, but are well navigated through practices that are learned through group intelligence that is cultivated over time. As such, we call these approaches "emergent practices," in contrast to the "best practices" more appropriate to Simple problems or the "better practices" of Complicated problems.

Chaotic Problems

One additional category is worth mentioning at this time: Chaotic problems are those for which we cannot discern a pattern, or for which the "rules of engagement" have yet to be defined, negotiated, and agreed upon by relevant parties. There are certain issues that naturally qualify within our corporate lives...[46]

> *For example, a new crisis has emerged in the organization related to larger, unpredicted political upheaval in the world. Our communication and decision-making channels and resources are otherwise committed, people are already busy with routine issues that align with our mission and strategic plan, etc. Suddenly, an emergency on the other side of the world disrupts our supply chain and delivery infrastructure.*

Upon further analysis, we find that we have practiced similar scenarios and have answered some of these challenges before. We can generally sort the Chaotic issues into sub-issues that fit the other categories, and then respond appropriately. This requires a nimble, flexible, and committed leadership and staff, but if we have practiced our Core Values and Intentions, we can be successful in such situations.

Assessment of Simple, Complicated, and Complex Problems in Practice

The assessment approaches we need to use should vary with the types of problems we are facing:

For Simple problems, the outcomes are readily measured and generally follow recognizable criteria – did the recipe taste good? Did it look appealing? Were ingredients used in proper proportion? Did the recipe stay on budget? These types of assessment questions make sense for Simple problems. Even in IT and Project Management, much of "requirements gathering" can use this approach and make sense: What does the customer need from the system? Is the solution addressing that need in a cost-effective way? Is the project following an understood timeline that accounts for input of all variables?

For Complicated problems, use of Logic Models can be extremely helpful in assessment, as they surface all relevant variables and how they are best utilized and sequenced to achieve preferred outcomes. If we are clear about the goal we seek to achieve, a process that uses formative and summative evaluation and assessment tools makes sense; Complicated problems fit this model beautifully.

But for Complex problems, another approach is required: We need to engage in frequent "pulse checks," sensing where the situation is now constructed and reformulating itself. This requires ongoing assessment, not only regarding anticipated outcomes, but also with sensitivity to new outcomes that are occurring.

> *For example, we might implement a new peer mentoring program at our company, hoping it will result in improved performance for those who are mentored. Of course, we count numbers of participants, hours involved, and basic levels of satisfaction with the program. BUT, if we are open to diverse metrics, we might discover (a) social impacts on mentors from being in a helping relationship, (b) shifts in work roles for mentors, now joining leadership of new projects, (c) higher engagement and retention rates for mentees, as their learning outcomes improve and they "catch on" and feel greater overall confidence in their work skills and connectedness to colleagues, or (d) that mentees return as mentors with future employees, seeking to "pay it forward" in gratitude.*

It isn't that these results **will occur**, but that they **may occur** and get noticed so there can be a more complete evaluation and understanding of the impacts of the program.

Complex problems benefit from "utilization-focused evaluation," an approach championed by Michael Quinn Patton (*Essentials of Utilization-Focused Evaluation*, 2011). This approach expressly allows us to treat innovation as an emergent process, one that respects its complexity, dynamism, and uncertainty. As such, we can pursue those strategies that become most promising (rather than having high certainty of them before starting the process), remaining flexible to notice new factors in the ever-changing currents of Complex challenges.

Exercise: Applied Assessment Using Patton's Model

WHO: Solo

WHY: To better understand how the various categories of challenges may be applied in practice, and how such insights may help align approaches that are appropriate to each type of issue.

HOW:

Step 1 - Using the Sorting Our Challenges Worksheet in Appendix B, identify an important workplace challenge you are facing. Sort its sub-issues into Simple, Complicated, Complex, and Chaotic "baskets" as a way to map your current understanding of the situation.

Step 2 - Then consider:

- Are we treating these issues appropriately?
- Are the right people involved in trying to address them?
- Are the people addressing these issues provided appropriate resource and training to address them successfully?
- Are we communicating appropriate expectations regarding each issue, given its nature?

In *Alice in Wonderland*, the Cheshire Cat told Alice, *"If you don't know where you are going, any road will get you there!"* To succeed with any significant change, people often need to know where they are headed and whether they are achieving desired results. I get that: Otherwise, they have no ability to discern whether their change efforts are progressing or adding any value. But in *some situations*, the goals are less discernible, the "roads" to traverse may be dusty paths, and trails are less travelled. By understanding whether we are dealing with Simple, Complicated, or Complex issues, we will gain necessary insights regarding how best to approach such change efforts, and have a far more interesting journey along the way.[47]

Synthesis: Attune to our Long-Term Intentions

Let's return to our original idea of Intention: Continuous attention to Intention is essential, requiring ongoing practice. In our current culture, we have a tendency to artificially compartmentalize our various projects and also separate Work from Life journeys. While some of this may be useful and appropriate, Intention unifies ways to relate distinct issues and shows us how to sustain healthy practices over time. Intention reminds us What Matters.

The commitment made to create a collaborative, innovative, healthy organization isn't something that can be viewed as the "flavor of the month." It is a sincere and thorough Intention to align our business practices with the things that matter to us and the betterment of the world. We spend vast portions of our lives in our workplaces, and our companies define much of the economic and social opportunity that we create as a society. We may be able to continue for a time in the current mode of operating, focused exclusively on short-term return and shareholder investment. But the challenges of our complex, global economy and the social, environmental, and political uncertainties of the world require that we develop and experiment with new ways of Being and Working, ways that invite our best capacities to address these challenges.

There is urgency in this message, to be sure. For example, climate change poses significant disruption of communities, nations, and industries as they grapple with its implications. Tens of millions of people face the prospect of uprooting their lives, facing increasing uncertainty regarding their futures. Many will lose their homes and livelihoods to fires, floods, soil erosion, and conflicts that arise out of government responses. At the same time, new opportunities arise for those attuned to such concerns: Providing innovative energy sources, developing sustainable architecture made of eco-friendly materials, offering refugees new places to settle and addressing labor shortages, and creating new modes of production and transportation that can help address the crises now faced all offer new business and social enterprise possibilities. For those who continue unsustainable development without accounting for climate change, or who move slowly in the face of such accelerating challenges, the perils of inaction and denial threaten to upend expectations of power and responsibility. This brings with it the possibility of major civil unrest, with its own implications for our economic, political, and social lives. Such is the nature of the times in which we live and work; to focus on What Matters offers important ways to make a positive contribution during such turbulent transitions.

Exercise: Return to Intention with New Insights

WHO: Solo

WHY: To get clear regarding how the various tools and practices we have learned serve our core Values and Intentions.

HOW: We close this section by noticing a few Questions that have arisen, new Intentions that are formulating, new Promising Practices that could possibly be applied to them...and then creating a simple set of "accountability mechanisms" from which to sustain commitment to responding to these opportunities:

What new Intentions have emerged for you, your team, and your organization?

- How do they align with those you expressed earlier in this process?
- What are some promising practices that have emerged as important to integrate into your work so these Intentions can have life and thrive?
- What barriers or challenges exist that reduce the likelihood of success in implementing such approaches?
- What resources and commitments are present to navigate these potential obstacles?

Take a moment to focus on YOU... What do YOU need in order to sustain this effort?

Launch the Journey

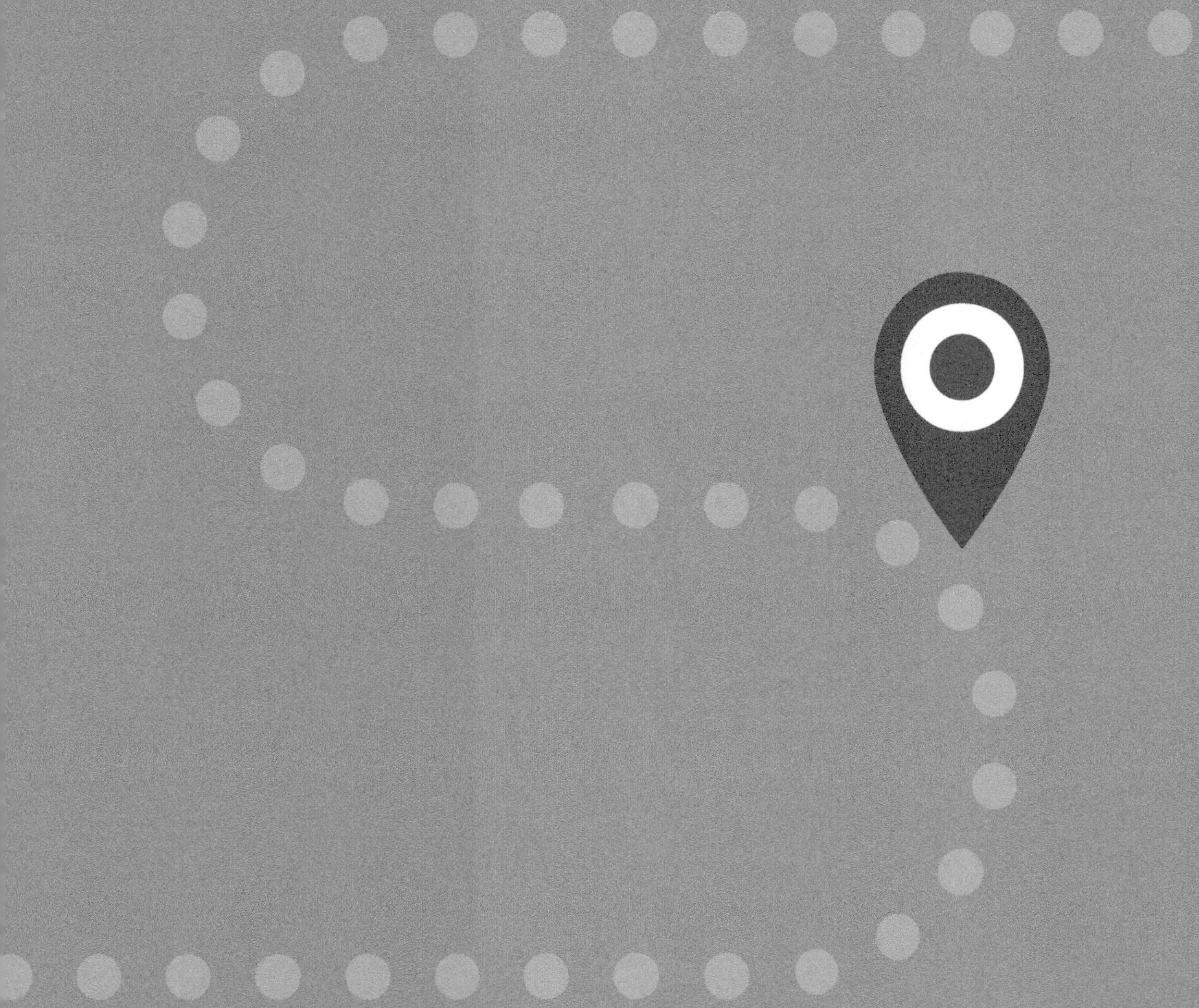

"Nothing is to be feared, it is only to be understood. Now is the time to understand more, so that we may fear less." – Marie Curie

In this section, we offer some additional tools and processes to practice, and then challenge you to utilize them. These Challenges are designed to help you apply what you have been learning to important questions that need to be addressed in your organization. They combine ideas that have been raised earlier with new insights that emerge from the lesson at hand.

There are four Challenges offered here: Take those that are timely and useful, and feel free to revisit earlier exercises and lessons that may reinforce your skills or improve your confidence. Of course, some of these approaches will feel "clunky" when they are new; allow yourself opportunities to learn from pilot experiences with sympathetic audiences. With experience, these approaches become second nature to practitioners, interwoven with usual business and meeting practices rather than being offered as "special workshops" or unique approaches to problem solving.

LESSON 28: COMMUNITY ENGAGEMENT USING "WORLD CAFE" AND "APPRECIATIVE INQUIRY"

"World Café Method," developed by David Isaacs and Juanita Brown, offers us a way to engage groups of varying sizes in meaningful deliberation and collaborative problem solving in a highly efficient manner. "Appreciative Inquiry", developed by David Cooperrider and colleagues at Case Western University, offers a strengths-based approach to conversations that reframes many of our usual assumptions about seeking "what's wrong" in a situation into finding "what's right" and energetically engaging people in a shared inquiry.[48] Appreciative Inquiry is anchored in its initial question of "provocative possibilities," challenging us to aspire to greatness and daring to pose questions that may be difficult to answer... it is a challenge worth taking.

This Challenge utilizes both approaches. Interestingly enough, we often do not label or name these processes when engaging them: We just "do it" and let the experience unfold. People marvel at how much they achieved, later to exclaim, *"So what was that process called that we just did? It worked really well!"* This lesson is for those seeking such tools!

Ever since its publication in 2005, *The World Café: Shaping our Futures Through Conversations that Matter* has been an important resource for facilitators and consultants across the globe. Authored primarily by Juanita Brown and David Isaacs, who have also led hundreds of workshops to teach this methodology, World Café offers a creative, collaborative, hospitable approach to deliberation. Participants in What Matters at Work are encouraged to delve more deeply into the details of the method. For our purposes here, I offer a basic approach that can be readily adapted to our Journey.

World Café

There are "Seven Principles" in World Café method that should be quickly understood:

Set the Context

Why are we meeting? Be really clear about this purpose, and then make sure those present are best able to achieve it: Are the right people in the room? Are we clear about what we seek from them? How will we get it?

Create Hospitable Space

We need a safe, inviting environment that encourages good, honest conversation. Many spaces aren't physically set-up to support this important element, so it may mean moving furniture or changing venues.

Explore Questions that Matter

Construct "powerful questions", that are worthy of people's time and effort. Be sure they generate energy from people by addressing them.

Encourage Full Participation

Create conversations so all can meaningfully engage: Build on their expertise and experience, use diverse modes of sharing, and take into account the power relationships in the room.

Connect Diverse Perspectives

By allowing movement around the room and reformulating new tables, "cliques" are broken and new communication patterns are formed. Hosts further facilitate sharing across mindsets, perhaps allowing some conversations that otherwise never take place in the organization.

Listen Together for Patterns

By modeling deep listening and encouraging it across all conversations, facilitators help others gain insights that would otherwise be elusive. Listening "between the lines" allows unspoken patterns to emerge and find voice.

Share Collective Discoveries

Conversations at each table are whole and have integrity. But this is just the beginning – find ways to harvest the many separate discussions and build collective connections, questions, answers, and other wisdom for follow-up and continued learning.

I have personally facilitated World Café processes with groups ranging up to four hundred people, but find that it is often a powerful revelation for groups as small as fifteen members. If we consider the Seven Principles in designing a meeting, the rewards in a brief amount of time can be staggering.[49]

Challenge A: Facilitate a World Café Experience

You're Ready for This!

WHO: Solo/Group

WHY: To experience World Café Method as a facilitator, applying it to a worthwhile and provocative issue that matters to you. This adaptation also infuses Appreciative Inquiry into the framing of questions.

HOW:

Step 1 - Start with a question that people can answer, perhaps having been prepared through a reading or prior activity. For example, in a leadership group, we might ask, "Recall a time when you experienced a profoundly positive example of leadership. Write down a brief story of where you were, what you noticed, and why it matters to you today." Give people a few minutes to silently reflect on the question, then share their stories with a Partner. (10 additional minutes, 5m per person)

Step 2 - Each person now goes to a different table, separate from your initial Partner. (5-6 people... can be up to 8 people): Together, briefly identify those Leadership Qualities that were most important in the stories they heard from their partners. One person at the table should scribe these Qualities on a flip chart, or on a piece of chart paper on the table. In the final five minutes, the group should identify two "key leadership qualities" they feel are most important to develop in the organization. (15-20m)

Step 3 - The Scribe remains at the table, while all additional group members redistribute themselves among the other tables in the room. Scribes can now think of themselves as Hosts, welcoming new members to the table. As people get settled at their new tables, welcome them and review the results of the previous conversation. New members are asked to offer any additional leadership qualities they feel improve the list at the new table, then the group identifies one such quality worthy of further discussion at this time. Host facilitates a new conversation: "How might we best develop this leadership quality so it may contribute to our organization's culture and efforts?" Record responses and contributions from all group members. Then, in the last few minutes, identify 2 "key approaches" that have come from the group. (20m)

Step 4 - Host remains at the table, and the groups switch one final time. Again, welcome newcomers and briefly review the results of previous discussion, into the final conversation topic. Discuss: "Looking at each of the two identified approaches - What are critical challenges that must be addressed in order to make this solution a reality?" (15m)

Step 5 - Hosts from the various tables post the results of their efforts on the walls around the room. Invite all participants to wander around the room, observing the various efforts and ideas now represented. Provide Post-It Notes and Sharpies so people may post comments, connections, and extensions to the ideas offered as they walk about the room (This is called a Gallery Walk). (10m... can go longer, especially if combined with a short break.)

Step 6 - Hold a (brief) large group conversation about what people have noticed in the results posted around the room. You may wish to use Focused Conversation Method (see the four levels of inquiry in Lesson 22) to get this feedback. Depending upon the nature of the exercise, you can now invite volunteers representing a diverse set of staff perspectives to work together to compile the results and develop a set of action steps to bring forward to management or back to the larger community for further refinement...

A Note: Organize a group to experience a World Café Process. It could be a staff team that wants to begin a conversation about its future direction, or a community of practice reflecting upon what now matters to its members. Whatever the focus, the conversation should be around a set of questions that matter, and which can bring forward the creative energies of those present.

This entire process can be completed in 90m, resulting in a significant amount of output from a diverse set of participants in your organization or community. It is an approach that integrates so much of what we have been learning, and with practice and familiarity, many organizations readily apply such tools as essential expectations of their policy-making, project management, and other decision-making processes.

With larger groups, more time should be allocated to realistically manage the logistics of the space. When addressing more complex questions, we advise utilizing trained facilitators at each table, rather than Hosts who emerge from the participants. In linguistically diverse settings, it may also be important to offer sessions where multiple languages are available for interpretation.

LESSON 29: PROBLEM-SOLVING AND THE "OUTCOMES IDENTIFICATION EXERCISE"

A key challenge occurs when we are invited to engage in longer planning, policy-making, or conflict negotiation processes without being adequately prepared to do so. One important contribution that you can make as a member of a group considering such efforts is to help group members first clarify What Matters, by identifying those things that reflect their values, Intentions, and expectations of one another in their work together. A simple process that we have utilized with great success is the "Outcomes Identification Exercise." I initially came across a variant of this activity in the Pfeiffer group facilitation *Annual* in 1987,[50] and we have adapted it to work with dozens of work units, community groups, and leadership teams preparing for strategic planning.

It is often useful at times of conflict and struggle, where there is a desire to move forward with planning or change efforts that have been stymied by relationships that have run aground. By clarifying the desired outcomes each participant seeks from work, and then noticing and affirming ways current efforts contribute to such intentions, members begin to learn (or re-learn) things about one another that can transform their energy and commitment. Once again, by focusing on strengths and assets within the group, the stage is set for important work that has otherwise eluded them.

Outcomes Identification Exercise - Process Overview

Facilitator's Opening Statement

"A key challenge facing people who need to work through conflicts together is a lack of clarity about what they need. Their expectations regarding how those needs are met, and the relative priority of these

expectations, is at the heart of this exercise. By clarifying desired outcomes from their work together, participants can begin to build an agenda that addresses those needs in practice."

Step 1: Silent Brainstorming

Individually, each participant should 'brainstorm' a list of responses to the following question:

"What outcomes do I desire from my workplace?"

An alternative question may be:

"What expectations do I have from my work with my co-workers?"

Take 5 minutes of quiet time to write down as many answers as possible to the focus question.

Step 2: Nominal Group Sharing

Going around the circle, each group* member should identify one desired outcome to share with others. The facilitator should record these responses on flip chart paper. Go around the circle a couple of times... if a 'desired outcome' has been previously stated, participants are encouraged to identify other items from their personal lists. People may "pass," if preferred. After completing 2-3 turns around the group, the facilitator should ask members to review the flip chart list and identify any other items from their personal lists that they now feel are important to add to the group list.

**At the end of this step, the group's list should contain 12-15 items. This assumes 5-7 members per group; if working with a larger group, it is advisable to break into subgroups.*

Step 3: Hear What Has Been Noticed

Elicit feedback from group members regarding the characteristics of the desired outcomes they now observe. Ask them (if not otherwise noted) to notice the relatively significant role of procedural and relational needs (See Lesson 21) identified in these lists. [If you have a few sub-groups, it may be helpful to have people 'wander around' and view the other lists before making these comments.]

Step 4: Affirm What Matters

Ask each person to reflect upon the group list that has been generated, as well as their personal lists. Then ask each group member to take 3 minutes to compose two statements:

A. *"One desired outcome I am working to achieve ______." This is very important to our work group because ______."*

B. *"I know that (someone else in the group or work team) is working to achieve (another desired outcome). This is very important to our work group because ______."*

Encourage group members to elaborate fully with these statements. Then, when all are ready, have people share them with one another, each in turn around the table.

**Again, small groups may be desirable. However, there is tremendous power in the experience of hearing people share these statements within the larger group. The facilitator should determine which approach is best in this situation.*

Step 5: From Ideas to Action (Optional)

Building an action agenda often flows from the listing of desired outcomes in Step 3. You may return to this list and ask participants to identify [with check marks or colored dots] the "top 3" items on the collective list that should now be acted upon by the group. After people are polled in this manner, the group should identify those priority items that now appear to be meaningful and actionable for the group, and set aside time to address those items in the best possible way.

NOTE: Since this exercise may be used as a training exercise, moving ahead to problem-solving may not be appropriate within this meeting. On other occasions, however, it is a natural next step.

Challenge B: Outcomes Identification Exercise

WHO: Solo/Group

WHY: To apply this process to a meaningful issue.

HOW:

Step 1 - Identify a group of colleagues that wants (or needs) to engage in a meaningful problem-solving process. This may be due to workplace challenges or difficulties, or it may come from a genuinely positive desire to improve their work together. Set aside 90 minutes for this conversation and facilitate the steps of the process outlined above - you can do this!

Step 2 - Follow the steps outlined above.

Step 3 - Later, (a) journal your insights and questions, then (b) discuss with a Coach or Mentor (perhaps someone engaging in this Journey with you) the power of the process and the results of the experience, and (c) reflect upon your own Values and Intentions and how they align with doing this work for you.

LESSON 30: CONFLICTS AND "HANDS ON MEDIATION"

In Lesson 23, we outlined a Conflict Resolution process that is useful for negotiating difficult issues with another person. We also offered a Collaborative Negotiation Process (Lesson 21), outlining steps to achieve solutions that address the underlying interests and concerns of all parties. In this next Challenge, we invite you to facilitate a conversation between two parties in conflict, working as a mediator with others within your organization. If we are to succeed in our Journey towards What Matters at Work, we need to address conflictive issues that weigh us down, cause people excessive stress, and derail us from the path. Indeed, many organizations suffer because talented individuals either leave for other companies or withdraw their energies while remaining, resigned to the reality that *"nothing will ever change as long as – is still here."*

Mediating such a conversation requires one to serve as an impartial third party, willing to set aside personal judgments or biases in order to facilitate and empower those engaged in the dispute.

You might assume this role because it naturally follows a position you hold, such as a team lead, supervisor, or Human Resources professional. But you might also offer to facilitate such a discussion because you have the respect of colleagues involved in the issues, and they trust your capacity to be impartial, respectful, and supportive of their efforts. In any event, your role is to be a calm and impartial third set of eyes and ears, supporting those in the dispute as they seek to understand one another and negotiate fair, balanced, and realistic agreements that allow them to work together.

It may be challenging to set aside biases and pre-judgments, or to resist the urge to offer suggested solutions - after all, you are a great problem-solver! With practice and respect for the process, you will find that serving as a supportive, listening presence is far more empowering to the individuals involved in the conflict.

"Hands-On Mediation" Process

We call this, "Hands On Mediation," and it follows the same principles as the processes outlined in our earlier work:

Phase 1: Pre-Negotiation

Meet individually and confidentially with each participant. Understand their needs and concerns, desired outcomes, and options in the situation. Clarify your role so they understand you are here to impartially facilitate, not to judge or decide results.

Phase 2: Opening

When bringing people together, start with an Opening Statement in order to establish ground rules and clarify the process. It can be informal, but gain agreement to ground rules.

Phase 3: Understanding the Conflict

Patiently allow each person to be heard, reflecting the underlying concerns being expressed. As appropriate, ask participants to restate what they are hearing from one another in order to demonstrate their commitment to listen fully and understand each other's perspectives.

Phase 4: Working it Out (Problem-Solving)

Summarize the issues that have been presented and the Agenda that has now emerged. Take one issue at a time, starting with those issues that all parties agree are important to address (start with a smaller issue, rather than the largest, most intractable one). Generate options, clarify criteria, and defer judgment as you explore possible responses to these concerns.

Phase 5: Agreement Development

Build an agreement that is mutually acceptable. There are no guarantees these actions will succeed, but there should be buy-in and a willingness to try them out. Use our "Hallmarks of a Good Agreement" to test the results.

Phase 6: Closing

Conclude the conversation with a genuine and positive statement of support for the efforts involved. Identify clear "next steps," including any follow-up meetings.

Challenge C: Hands-On Mediation

WHO: Group

WHY: To apply the mediation process and previously learned negotiation and conflict management skills to a workplace dispute as an impartial third party.

HOW:

Step 1 - Identify one of the Scenarios from Appendix A to use as practice. Follow the Steps outlined above.

Step 2 - Debrief with participants so all can learn from the experience. Practice other Scenarios, as appropriate, to gain fluency and confidence with the process.

Step 3 - As previously suggested, journal your insights and questions, then discuss with a Coach or Mentor (perhaps someone engaging in this Journey with you) on the power of the process and the results of the experience. Reflect upon your own Values and Intentions and how they align with doing this work for you.

Impasse may be experienced - this is normal. Be prepared to return to an earlier phase of the process or to take a break to check in with participants. If you are able to remain calm, positive, and patient, you encourage such behavior in others.

When applying this approach to real disputes, be sure to follow up with each participant in a few days, in case any clarification is needed or unresolved issues continue to fester. Such a "check in" allows you to bring people together as needed to prevent new issues from escalating.

LESSON 31: MANAGE TRANSITIONS WITH THE COMMUNITY

One of the important leadership challenges of What Matters is to help others navigate change at a variety of levels: We need to address changes in our staff teams, organizational strategic priorities, resources available to deliver services, the technologies we utilize in our work, or changes in the larger political and social contexts in which we operate. While much has been written on the subject of change management (most notably the work of Joseph Kotter[52]), and we have taken Rolf Smith's change model and integrated it into our Core Story (see Lesson 4), there is another dimension that gets far less attention but which is equally important: Transition.

Transition is the process of addressing the internal responses people experience to the external changes around them. Most notably addressed by William Bridges *Managing Transitions* (1991, 2017), *The Way of Transition*, (2001) and other writings, transitions offer us an excellent window into the reasons people resist change or otherwise find changes difficult to accept.

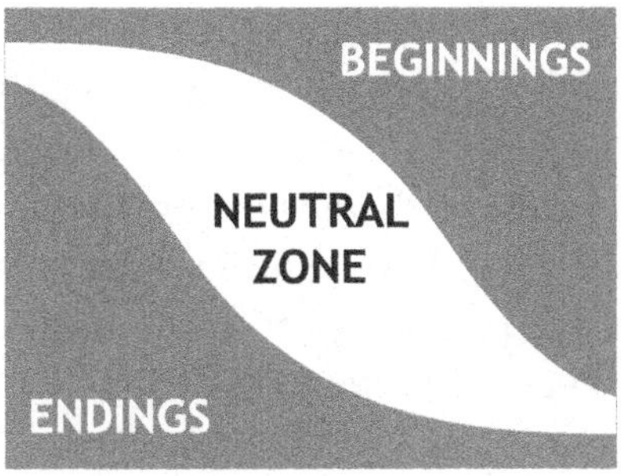

Bridges Transitions Model

Bridges identifies three phases of transition:

Endings occur when we are concluding or leaving a previous set of relationships and practices. These include all categories of concerns (see Lesson 21 on Collaborative Negotiation), and they occur both in anticipation of the "end date" and in the days and weeks that follow it.

The **Neutral Zone** is that time when we feel uncertain and uprooted. We are no longer anchored by the "good old days" when we understood our roles and direction, and are not yet confident in the ways of the future. People often feel anxious at such times, and lack confidence that they have a place or relationships they can trust. This is a liminal period of time for staff, customers, and leaders; all are attempting to navigate the changes, but they aren't fully integrated into the new procedures.

Beginnings start as we approach the transition date, and accelerate over time as we adopt new systems, develop new relationships, and begin new projects and services that once were seen as "future state" in our planning processes. Beginnings can be exciting for some, nerve-wracking for others; they don't simply occur because we have "flipped the switch" on the new organization or systems.

For example, let's say we are concluding a project that has served our clients for several years. Those clients must either make the transition to a new service, or go without such service. The staff who provided the service must also adjust to no longer being employed in the previous manner; they either move on to new projects (perhaps with very different colleagues) or leave the organization entirely. People often move to new work spaces, change schedules, stop working with certain important colleagues or clients, and start new relationships.

Using Bridges' model, one can easily imagine the range of feelings and perspectives that surround this transition, and the opportunities to go astray from those things that matter to staff, clients, and the larger organization. Yet all too often, leaders focus on minimizing these experiences: They focus on completing tasks and telling people to simply accept that we aren't in the previous state of operation any longer. Resentments build, often expressed "underground" rather than in open meetings, and those who raise questions are labeled as "resisting change" and not being "team players." Information is often withheld by leadership during such transitions, for fear that providing imperfect information will cause stress. They haven't quite figured out what will occur and don't want staff and customers acting on matters that haven't been decided.

Paradoxically, we need to do the opposite of what usually occurs: We need to fully and transparently engage staff, customers, and other stakeholders in meaningful conversations about What Matters. If we are going to sustain trust and integrity with these critical partners in the change process, we must embrace the normal experiences of anger, fear, and uncertainty - as well as the aspects of excitement, elation, and anticipation - that are understood through the lens of transition.[53]

As we engage in such discussions, we need to do so in a manner that aligns processes with our goals, promises, and priorities. This is well-expressed in the work of the International Association for Public Participation (IAP2), one of the pre-eminent facilitation professional organizations in the world. IAP2 offers a "Spectrum of Public Participation" that helps us clearly see how we must align these factors:[54]

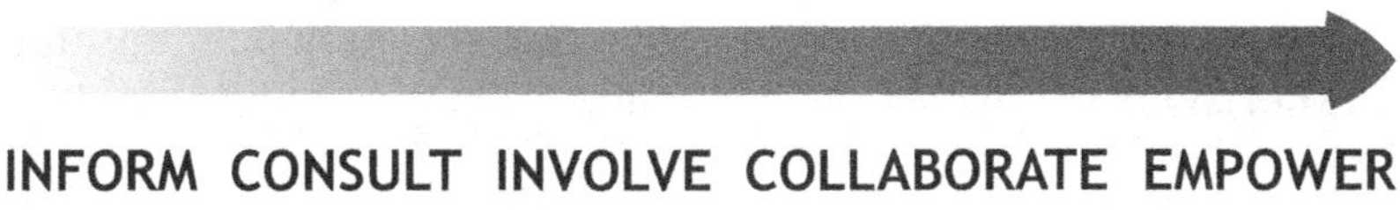

IAP2 Spectrum of Public Participation

Inform

Public participation goal: To provide the public with balanced and objective information to assist them in understanding the problem, alternatives, opportunities and/or solutions.

Promise to the public: We will keep you informed.

Consult

Public participation goal: To obtain public feedback on analysis, alternatives and/or decisions.

Promise to the public: We will keep you informed, listen to and acknowledge concerns and aspirations, and provide feedback on how public input influenced the decision. We will seek your feedback on drafts and proposals.

Involve

Public participation goal: To work directly with the public throughout the process to ensure that public concerns and aspirations are consistently understood and considered.

Promise to the public: We will work with you to ensure that your concerns and aspirations are directly reflected in the alternatives developed and provide feedback on how public input influenced the decision.

Collaborate

Public participation goal: To partner with the public in each aspect of the decision including the development of alternatives and the identification of the preferred solution.

Promise to the public: We will work together with you to formulate solutions and incorporate your advice and recommendations into the decisions to the maximum extent possible.

Empower

Public participation goal: To place final decision-making in the hands of the public.

Promise to the public: We will implement what you decide.

Challenge D: Manage Transitions with Community Engagement

WHO: Solo/Group/Organization

WHY: To focus on transition as a key organizational challenge... here is your next Challenge. It is going to take awhile, but it synthesizes several processes and skill sets we have practiced previously. As a result, your community or organization may experience a profound shift in the way people are engaged in important transitions going forward.

HOW:

Step 1 - Focus on a change effort that is planned in the coming weeks. If none is already contemplated, take time to bring a group together to consider what might be such a change that is needed.

Step 2 - Consider carefully:

- What are the desired outcomes of this change effort? What do you understand to be he opportunities and costs of this change?
- What might be some ways Staff, customers, and other stakeholders might experience transitions related to this change? On what data or insights do you base your conclusions - where might be your biases or blind spots that limit this understanding?
- How might we best engage our "public" in order to fully understand and appreciate their knowledge, insights, and experiences related to the planned (or proposed) change?

Step 3 - Using the IAP2 Spectrum as a guide: Design an engagement process that aligns with your responses to the above questions. Utilize approaches otherwise outlined and practiced in this Guide.

Step 4 - With a team of facilitators representing diverse perspectives on the issue, seek to fully understand the perspectives of those impacted. Do so in a manner that is timely, respectful, inclusive, and honest... or otherwise stays true to your Values and Intentions about What Matters at Work.

Step 5 - Debrief, reflect, and learn... this is a continuous process of learning and improvement.

Congratulations! You have now launched your Journey and navigated some initial Challenges that are essential to What Matters! Working to mediate conflicts, engage groups in creative problem-solving, manage transitions, and define desired outcomes are important to efforts to align our Intentions and Core Values with those of our organization. Utilizing facilitative leadership skills and processes such as those deployed in this section greatly improves participant engagement and capacities to address the right issues in the best possible ways. Now that we've come this far, we need to examine how to sustain ourselves through deepened learning.

Learn Together to Deepen Capacity

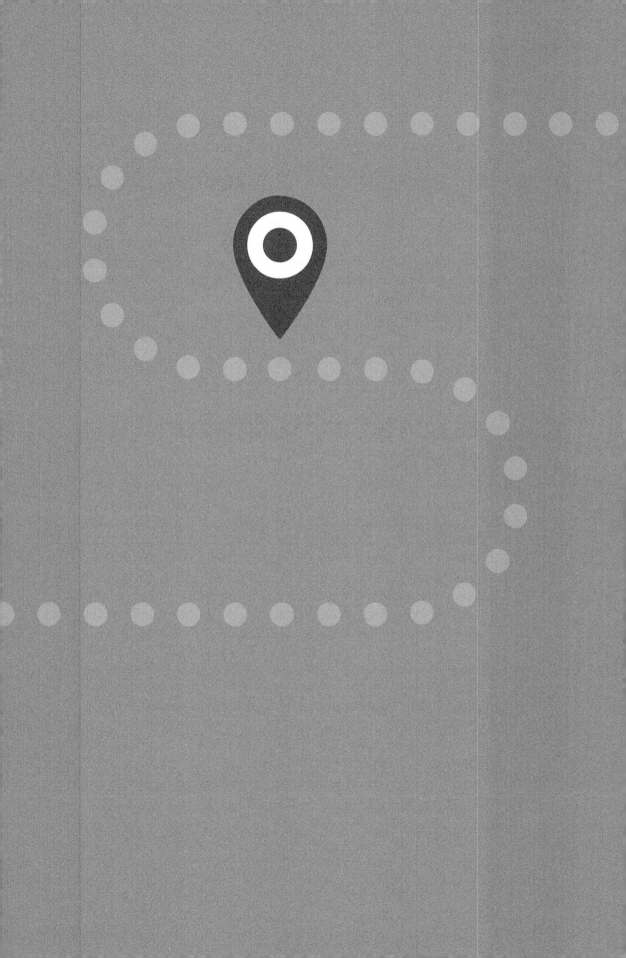

There are many tools at our disposal, but ultimately the search for What Matters comes down to our capacity to find it, retain it in our focus, and sustain it in our work. This section offers two important resources to develop and maintain that capacity: Communities of Practice are vibrant, empowering learning models that facilitate trust-based relationships and transform otherwise independent, competitive approaches into collaborative centers of knowledge sharing, experimentation, and learning. Servant-Leadership offers a natural pathway to capacity building throughout the organization, all in service to What Matters. Together, they help us bridge our thinking into sustainable action.

LESSON 32: COMMUNITIES OF PRACTICE

Communities of Practice (CoP's) are peer-organized, self-directed learning groups that bring together those who share an interest across an organization (or beyond such boundaries). CoP's build collaborative skills and knowledge-sharing based upon trust and cohesiveness, and do so in remarkably cost-effective ways. Not only are they intrinsically powerful and beneficial to their members, but CoP's build relationships among diverse constituencies and world views. I've been fortunate to work with many CoP's over the past twenty years, and they are truly central to the practices we are discussing here. Foremost among theorists and writers in this area is Etienne Wenger,[55] who has identified three core elements of these types of learning communities:

Domain

This is the area of focus or the core challenge that members are seeking to address through their learning and meeting together.

Community

This relates to the relationship building, trust development, communication practices and identity transformation that occurs within the CoP.

Practice

This is how the CoP enhances the skills and knowledge of members so they can test and apply what they have learned to the practical challenges of their work.

All CoP's need to pay attention to domain, community, and practice elements in order to sustain themselves and offer contributions to the organizations in which they are embedded. Paradoxically, such attention needs to start with Community, as the trust developed among members is fundamental to a willingness to define a meaningful set of Practice opportunities within a well-defined Domain. Members bring real challenges, taking the risk to be vulnerable regarding what they don't understand or what frightens them, and then generously offer practical strategies to safely address those issues. CoP's are also excellent spaces for sharing recent learning, as we have previously mentioned; sharing conference materials and connections, teaching key lessons from workshops attended, testing new language for policies, etc. These ideas all gain a receptive audience that gives needed critique before taking them further into implementation.

While management may play a catalyzing role in convening a CoP, the energy for sustaining it must come from its members. This poses a natural tension, as management understandably seeks to align the agenda and activities of staff with the goals and mission of the company, and some activities within a CoP may not necessarily come together in that manner. This is where strong communication is required between CoP leadership and formal leadership, supporting staff participation while not directing it. There are tangible ways management can express this support without undermining the independence and self-determination of the CoP: Staff often need explicit statements of support for CoP participation from their supervisors, and need channels to convey learning back to colleagues in team meetings to validate such participation and maximize its benefits.

In my experience, management can also facilitate broader communication of ideas and concerns that emerge from CoP meetings: Central leadership can provide for the occasional financial needs of CoP groups as they engage in programs that benefit members or communicate their learning across the organization. While such needs are modest, the symbolic and tangible value of support can come at critical times.

The HR-Communities of Practice Office at the University of Wisconsin-Madison

(A Success Story)

I had the privilege of serving as founding Director of an innovative office that continues to develop creative leadership and skills development using a CoP approach. In the follow-up to a fundamental redesign of the Human Resources system at the University of Wisconsin, the HR-CoP Office was established. Its charge was to facilitate the training required to shift from a highly centralized, transactional approach to HR to one that is decentralized and relational in nature, all while nearly 900 HR and Payroll professionals at the University continued to assure that everyone received their paychecks, benefits, and accurate resolution of the varied technical challenges faced on a daily basis.

We adopted a unique community of practice approach because the new system required development of trusting, transparent, and honest relationships in a manner that had not generally existed. We also knew that many of the key members of the HR community needed to play leadership roles in gaining the engagement of colleagues, both within HR and in many other key administration sectors of this vast bureaucracy. Through the excellent work of Sarah Carroll and Joshua Schwab, the HR-CoP office quickly developed a wide array of learning experiences, both online and face-to-face, all within a creative competency-based model that Sarah crafted in consultation with the HR community. These included mastery of the required technical knowledge, to be sure, but also the important interpersonal skills needed in this new approach. Competencies were articulated in change management, collaboration, communication, ethics and integrity, problem-solving, and technical competencies, all grounded in competency in diversity and inclusion that serves as fundamental to the entire enterprise.

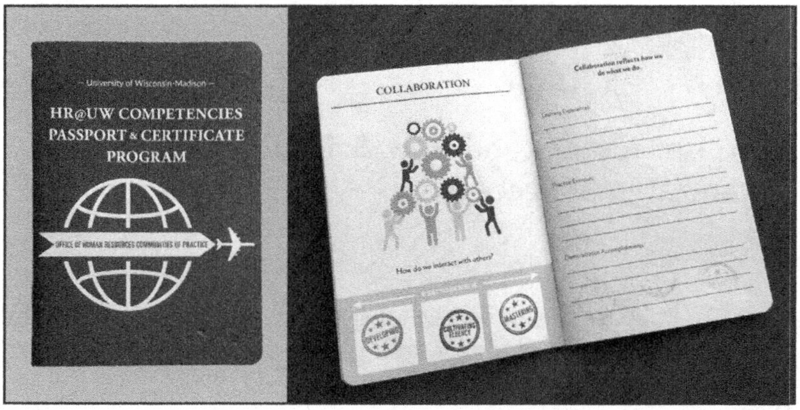

HR@UW Competencies Passport

Over the past four years, several hundred staff have now successfully engaged in this effort, participating in Learning Cohorts that meet for three months to learn how to apply these competencies to their work. The approach is illustrated by this Passport, demonstrating the learner's journey through various levels of knowledge and skill in each competency area.[56] In addition, HR-CoP staff support others across campus as they convene learning communities that address timely policy challenges and facilitate knowledge transfer across the organization. It is a true collaboration in process and substance.

The sustained commitment of the HR-CoP Office demonstrates how the various skills and strategies we've been discussing can be scaled up and implemented while remaining true to Core Values and Intentions.[57] They have created an empowering program that engages hundreds of people, requiring diverse technical knowledge (e.g., benefits, labor relations, recruitment, international visas). HR-CoP utilizes a peer-led educational model that builds upon the Kolb Learning Cycle (Lesson 17), development evaluation (Lesson 27), and a full commitment to a diverse and inclusive workplace (Lesson 18). This approach all occurs within a traditional bureaucracy with strict requirements regarding security, confidentiality, labor contracts, and transactional accuracy, demonstrating how to achieve these technical requirements while valuing trust-based, transparent relationships.

Exercise: Understand How CoP's Contribute to Organizational Success

WHO: Solo

WHY: To improve our understanding of the outcomes of CoP's by examining empirical evidence and stories from an organization.

HOW:

Step 1 - One way to better understand and appreciate the possibilities associated with starting a CoP is to review this engaging report and presentation by Bethany Laursen from 2015, in which she evaluated the impacts of several CoP's that I convened at the time: www.talent.wisc.edu and then search "CoP Impact Evaluation Report."

Step 2 - After doing so, consider your own organization: What possibilities exist to establish or otherwise support a CoP where you work?

Step 3 - Download the free CoP Design Guide created by members of the UW-Madison CoP Network (www.talent.wisc.edu), then search for "CoP Design Guide" and use it as a resource to guide your efforts. Keep in mind your broader Journey here, your efforts to identify "What Matters'" and the larger context of our learning here.

LESSON 33: DEVELOP LEADERSHIP THROUGHOUT THE ORGANIZATION

"Allow those you lead... To lead... when they feel the need. All will benefit." - Gordon MacKenzie, Orbiting the Giant Hairball (1998)

Organizations often offer leadership development opportunities only to new managers and supervisors, top executives seen as "most important" for such investment, or perhaps "young leaders" being tapped for future management roles. But this approach reflects a parochial perspective on leadership, one that inappropriately equates *leadership* with *management*. I am continually impressed with companies that have decoupled such approaches, recognizing that managers at various stages of their careers and levels of development have one set of needs, and that people can offer leadership across the organization in a variety of roles. Developing such leadership capacities is at the heart of this practice.

Transformative leadership development is informed by several theories that are worth further exploration, including the work of Covey, Senge, Wheatley, Scharmer, Bennis, Jaworski, and Greenleaf.[58] You will find that these theories are consistent in so many ways with the best practices, values, and strategies encouraged here: The key at this point is to consider how they may be faithfully integrated into your organization.

A few practices worth consideration:

Create a leadership development certificate as a unique program within your company's efforts in Talent Management. Separating leadership from management allows a broader swath of staff to engage in such learning, both because they volunteer to do so and because their managers and supervisors might offer such opportunities as elements of goal setting and career progression. Use Enlightened Assessment approaches that are personalized to learners, where they demonstrate leadership competencies in a way that aligns with Core Values and individual learner needs. Certificates should reflect how learning demonstrates these competencies at basic, intermediate, and advanced levels of proficiency. Certificate holders can then be tapped for special leadership opportunities within the organization, facilitating engagement and deliberation among staff or leading project teams and task forces; such opportunities give the certificate "currency" in the company's own valuation system and can be ways to retain some of the best staff in the company.

Create an advanced leadership seminar, intended for those who have completed the basic certificate requirements, where participants focus on key leadership issues they are facing in their work. Utilize "graduates" of the seminar as peer mentors to support the next cohort, thus reinforcing the value of the experience by guiding others in the manner they were once guided. This two-phase process is very powerful for all participants, and it sets the stage for an ongoing learning community that can serve as a "room of requirement" (to use a Harry Potter term[59]) when crises are noticed and need a diverse set of perspectives to address them.[60]

Engage top leadership in these learning efforts, teaching sessions where they have expertise, and otherwise acknowledging core learning milestones experienced by those involved in these experiences. We have used the peer mentoring experience as the basis for a "capstone" meeting with top leaders in the above example, resulting in great insights for all involved and, on occasion, direct action to address broadly important issues.

Support workshops, aside from any certificates, that enhance skills in leadership-related practices. These might include work in facilitation, conflict resolution, collaborative negotiation, creative problem-solving, systems thinking, conducting "crucial conversations," and related topics (many of which we have explored here). Create ongoing opportunities for learning, shared in a variety of contexts, and use workshops as catalysts for conversations that apply the learning. We need to resist the antiquated notion that learning is separated bureaucratically from application, and integrate skills and insights into the spaces where work gets done.

Among the theories involved in constructing such a program is the concept of Servant-Leadership, first articulated by Robert Greenleaf in 1970 in his essay, *"The Servant as Leader,"* and since expanded upon by Larry Spears and others in an impressive collection of books, essays, and other resources. One of Larry Spears' essays, *"10 Characteristics of a Servant-Leader"* (1992) offers those core qualities of leadership that are essential. These are included as Spears defines them:

Listening

Leaders have traditionally been valued for their communication and decision-making skills. Although these are also important skills for the servant-leader, they need to be reinforced by a deep commitment to listening intently to others. The servant-leader seeks to identify the will of a group and helps to clarify that will. He or she listens receptively to what is being said and unsaid. Listening also encompasses hearing one's own inner voice. Listening, coupled with periods of reflection, is essential to the growth and well-being of the servant-leader.

Empathy

The servant-leader strives to understand and empathize with others. People need to be accepted and recognized for their special and unique spirits. One assumes the good intentions of co-workers and colleagues and does not reject them as people, even when one may be forced to refuse to accept certain behaviors or performance. The most successful servant-leaders are those who have become skilled empathetic listeners.

Healing

The healing of relationships is a powerful force for transformation and integration. One of the great strengths of servant-leadership is the potential for healing one's self and one's relationship to others. Many people have broken spirits and have suffered from a variety of emotional hurts. Although this is a part of being human, servant-leaders recognize that they have an opportunity to help make whole those with whom they come in contact. In his essay, *The Servant as Leader*, Greenleaf writes, "There is something subtle communicated to one who is being served and led if, implicit in the compact between servant-leader and led, is the understanding that the search for wholeness is something they share."

Awareness

General awareness, and especially self-awareness, strengthens the servant- leader. Awareness helps one in understanding issues involving ethics, power and values. It lends itself to being able to view most situations from a more integrated, holistic position. As Greenleaf observed: "Awareness is not a giver of solace--it is just the opposite. It is a disturber and an awakener. Able leaders are usually sharply awake and reasonably disturbed. They are not seekers after solace. They have their own inner serenity."

Persuasion

Another characteristic of servant-leaders is reliance on persuasion, rather than on one's positional authority, in making decisions within an organization. The servant-leader seeks to convince others, rather than coerce compliance. This particular element offers one of the clearest distinctions between the traditional authoritarian model and that of servant-leadership. The servant-leader is effective at building consensus within groups. This emphasis on persuasion over coercion finds its roots in the beliefs of the Religious Society of Friends (Quakers)--the denominational body to which Robert Greenleaf belonged.

Conceptualization

Servant-leaders seek to nurture their abilities to dream great dreams. The ability to look at a problem or an organization from a conceptualizing perspective means that one must think beyond day-to-day realities. For many leaders, this is a characteristic that requires discipline and practice. The traditional leader is consumed by the need to achieve short-term operational goals. The leader who wishes to also be a servant-leader must stretch his or her thinking to encompass broader-based conceptual thinking. Within organizations, conceptualization is, by its very nature, a key role of boards of trustees or directors.

Unfortunately, boards can sometimes become involved in the day-to-day operations – something that should be discouraged –and thus fail to provide the visionary concept for an institution. Trustees need to be mostly conceptual in their orientation, staff members are operational in their perspective, and the most effective executive leaders probably need to develop both perspectives within themselves. Servant-leaders are called to seek a delicate balance between conceptual thinking and a day-to-day operational approach.

Foresight

Closely related to conceptualization, the ability to foresee the likely outcome of a situation is hard to define, but easier to identify. One knows foresight when one experiences it. Foresight is a characteristic that enables the servant-leader to understand the lessons from the past, the realities of the present, and the likely consequence of a decision for the future. It is also deeply rooted within the intuitive mind. Foresight remains a largely unexplored area in leadership studies, but it deserves careful attention.

Stewardship

Peter Block (author of *Stewardship and The Empowered Manager*) has defined stewardship as "holding something in trust for another." Robert Greenleaf's view of all institutions was one in which CEO's, staff members, and trustees all played significant roles in holding their institutions in trust for the greater good of society. Servant-leadership, like stewardship, assumes first and foremost a commitment to serving the needs of others. It also emphasizes the use of openness and persuasion, rather than control.

Commitment to the Growth of People

Servant-leaders believe that people have an intrinsic value beyond their tangible contributions as workers. As such, the servant- leader is deeply committed to the growth of each and every individual within his or her organization. The servant-leader recognizes the tremendous responsibility to do everything in his or her power to nurture the personal and professional growth of employees and colleagues. In practice, this can include (but is not limited to) concrete actions such as making funds available for personal and professional development, taking a personal interest in the ideas and suggestions from everyone, encouraging worker involvement in decision-making, and actively assisting laid-off employees to find other positions.

Building Community

The servant-leader senses that much has been lost in recent human history as a result of the shift from local communities to large institutions as the primary shaper of human lives. This awareness causes the servant-leader to seek to identify some means for building community among those who work within a given institution. Servant-leadership suggests that true community can be created among those who work in businesses and other institutions. Greenleaf said, "All that is needed to rebuild community as a viable life form for large numbers of people is for enough servant-leaders to show the way, not by mass movements, but by each servant-leader demonstrating his or her unlimited liability for a quite specific community-related group."

Exercise: Servant-Leadership and What Matters

WHO: Solo

WHY: To understand how qualities of Servant-Leadership are applied (or not) to your organization, and to consider the implications for What Matters.

HOW:

Step 1 - Reflect on these questions:

How are these qualities developed, supported, and applied within your organization?

- Which qualities are most valued in your organization? Which are less valued?
- From your perspective, which of these qualities are most important to express leadership so that What Matters emerges and aligns with your organization's needs?

Step 2 - Look for an opportunity to do ***one thing*** to enhance development of any of these characteristics. You might consider only your own work team or the larger context, whatever makes sense.

EPILOGUE: WHAT MATTERS AT LIFE

"I have walked through many lives,
some of them my own,
and I am not who I was,
though some principle of being abides,
from which I struggle not to stray."
- Stanley Kunitz, "The Layers" (1978)[61]

As we navigate our life journeys, we define ourselves in terms of numerous forms of Identity. We identify as members of our families of origin, as sons and daughters, sisters and brothers, only later to become life partners, parents, and grandparents. We identify in terms of our religious congregations, our social networks, and as members of ethnic groups that have passed on traditions for generations, centuries, even millennia. As we navigate these various forms of Identity, we don't necessarily shed our previous incarnations. Rather, as the poet Stanley Kunitz conveys in his poem, "The Layers," we seek to "live in the layers, not on the litter" of our lives. There are multiple layers and frames of Identity, with Work Identity being but one among many that matter to us.[62]

As I have experienced the transition from living in the United States to life in Canada, or from full-time employment to "semi-retirement," I have undergone a profound reflection in terms of my own multiple Identity frames. I still see myself as holding true to several of these forms of Identity at work, in my social circle, and in the broader society. While certain circles of Identity recede as I move through the layers, others gain greater prominence.

I must confess: Personally, I prefer spending significant amounts of time on my own, organizing my work and implementing it according to my own sense of priority and sequence. I tend to resist getting dragged into purposeless meetings or doing tedious work that is merely intended to protect political actors wearing bigger "hats" than I wear in that context. But I also relish meaningful interactions, especially with intelligent, dedicated people who see things I don't see and who have skills in areas critical to our success. I also value being with others who struggle and who want to do well, but who feel frustration and confusion. I appreciate and respect their struggle, and know that often I have things to contribute to the conversation that help them transcend their challenges and barriers. Sometimes, my value simply comes from being a Listening Presence, one who helps others make sense of their own challenges and opportunities. Other times, I have Facilitative Processes to offer, so I can help structure their interactions and channel their energies for Good. And still other times, I can be a Knowledgeable Resource (sometimes called a Subject Matter Expert), where my expertise can recognize patterns among the chaos and discern pathways towards useful solutions.

An irony of our current era is the paradox of connectedness. We are technologically connected as never before, able to have 24/7 access to the lives of billions of people and for the channels of communication to be networked more democratically than ever in history. For the privileged with access to such tools, there are vast opportunities for interactions, with huge social, economic, and political consequences, and there are ways to be positive forces in the world that were unimaginable only a few decades ago. But at the same time (without getting into the disparities of access in this network of connectedness), we also notice higher levels of anomie than ever previously recorded: So many feel alone, depressed, isolated, and marginalized, with relationships often at superficial levels that result in great senses of despair. You may recall we discussed this back in our conversation about physical spaces and What Matters (Lesson 11); I see profound implications for other dimensions of our lives beyond work.

The society in which many of us reside is one of rapid motion and immediate responses. There is relatively little opportunity for reflection, in-depth discussion, and the formation of trusting relationships so essential to navigating the complex challenges of the day. In the United States and much of the developed world, this is compounded by an economic system that increasingly accrues benefits and power to those with the greatest current wealth and power, and a political system designed in many ways to reinforce and protect these incentives. There is a great American story of upward mobility, of immigrants achieving a better life; while there are elements of truth in this myth, there are also significant systemic and cultural barriers that are powerful and growing more entrenched. There are also long-standing sources of pain and privilege that invisibly permeate the social fabric, and these have real implications for addressing any opportunities to change the ways we resolve them.

This is important to name and acknowledge here, because any of the suggestions captured in this book run headlong into such cultural and systemic realities. The ideal of a democratic workplace has always been at odds with the dominant paradigm; what is less readily understood is that the factors mitigating against such values being implemented are in many ways stronger today because of these political realities.

Still, there is hope: The same technologies that organize us in isolating, superficial ways can be channeled towards improved collaboration, meaningful problem identification, and negotiated solutions based upon What Matters. I find immense responsiveness to the opportunity to have trusting relationships and meaningful learning at work. Indeed, I would say most people take to such approaches like plants to water (of course, you have to be wary of becoming saturated!). If we mimic natural approaches, we tend to create systems that naturally replicate, self-nourish, and reasonably negotiate relationships with colleagues sharing territory and responsibilities.[63] The key is to have awareness of such needs, and then to clarify a strong Intention that supports taking actions consistent with this awareness.

What about You, fellow Journeyer? What does it mean for your life? Any of these aspects of Identity and ways of being useful in your work can be channeled in service to What Matters. In turn, you can be such a resource to your colleagues and your organization. It all goes back to the ideas discussed at the beginning of this Learning Journey:

- Intention helps us set the course,
- Values help us understand the milestones we will meet along the way,
- Processes and Practices help us navigate effectively as we endeavor to stay the course.
- Tools are known to us, residing in the backpacks we are carrying on the Journey: As we face the challenges along the road, we can pull them out and apply them to address those challenges.

That's it. That's What Matters at Work. Thank you for your dedication and commitment to get this far. May our efforts continue and reap bountiful harvests.

SPECIAL OFFER TO READERS!

As a way of expressing appreciation to our initial readers, we extend this opportunity: Would you like to have a free, 45m phone consultation with Harry? Send an email to harry.whatmatters@gmail.com requesting a session. Include in the Subject line **the last two words from the title** of Lesson 14. Offer good through June 30, 2020, dependent upon availability.

END NOTES

1. For a truly wonderful guide to such thinking and its meaning in the world of work, I suggest Gordon MacKenzie's, *Orbiting the Giant Hairball* (1998), with thanks to Christine Ray for first showing it to me. MacKenzie playfully demonstrates how to survive with creativity and integrity within a corporate culture that suffocates individual expression and demands conformity. If we "orbit" and resist getting sucked into the "hairball," we can maintain the energy and commitment required to help our organizations thrive in the midst of overwhelming pressures. One important aspect of "orbiting" for me has been maintaining flexibility over where I do certain work, often over cups of coffee in "third spaces" that facilitate creative, flexible thinking about challenging issues. The change of scenery actually opens up new channels for analyzing and discussing entrenched problems, so I return to my desk with renewed focus and commitment to the project at hand. "Wanderings" help us center, rediscover What Matters, and achieve great things.

2. Excerpted from David Whyte, *Crossing the Unknown Sea: Work as a Pilgrimage of Identity* (2001), found at www.awakin.org website.

3. I'm referring here to McGregor's theory of management and work motivation from the 1950's, organized in his book, *The Human Side of Enterprise* (1960). Less known is Abraham Maslow's work on "Theory Z" that offered another type of worker motivation, one premised on cultivating creativity, imagination, and moral excellence. When we consider What Matters, we might want to examine Maslow's thinking, as well.

4. Daniel Bell, *The Coming of Post-Industrial Society* (1974) coined the term that has now become synonymous with the service economy in which we now live. He foretold numerous transitions in economic production and transformations in the core relationships and institutions of our globalized economic system. Another excellent resource from this time period was Bennis and Slater, *The Temporary Society* (1968), which expressed the uncertainties of the times we were then entering, as well as the accelerating pace of change.

5. W. Brian Arthur, "Increasing Returns and the New World of Business, *Harvard Business Review*, July-Aug 1996.

6. As in the previous note, I believe this is what Maslow had in mind with Theory Z. In my own teaching and practice, I often remind people that What Matters to them is often first experienced in the Heart, an instinctive feeling that defies words. It is only after experiencing that *"Hazzah!"* epiphany we begin to contemplate what we want to do (Head) and how we want to do it (Hand). This aligns perfectly with Simon Sinek's "Golden Circle" model on starting with Why (see the next Lesson) with your Core Story.

7. Simon Sinek has created a simple format that is highly accessible. He calls it, "The Golden Circle." His *"Start With Why"* talk at *TEDx-Puget Sound* (2009) and subsequent book (2011) provide cogent explanations and illustrations of the approach, which I have adapted to use in my own teaching.

8. Otto Scharmer and his colleagues at MIT's Presencing Institute (*Theory U,* 2009) teach a process called, "generative listening." We adapt it here into a simpler exercise.

9. Margaret Wheatley, *Leadership and the New Science*, 1992. In my conversations with her, we have found much to build upon this idea.

10. Brian Robertson, *Holacracy: The New Management System for a Rapidly Changing World* (2015). Zappos has adopted this highly participatory decision-making model, and it is a story well worth reviewing; see their version of the story at www.zapposinsights.com/about/holacracy. Another innovative resource in this area is Galbraith, Downey, and Kates, *Designing Dynamic Organizations* (2001), which challenges us to consider alternative structures and reward systems within existing systems.

11. Kaner, *Facilitator's Guide to Participatory Decision-Making, 3rd Edition* (2014) is an excellent resource. His "diamond decision model" offers a simple illustration of a preferred approach, and his agenda templates can be applied to many business and community settings.

12. A free download of *Digital Habitats* is now available. It may be accessed at: www.technologyforcommunities.com – Especially useful is the "Action Notebook," which allows you to assess the status, orientation, and needs of your particular learning community.

13. See Meyer and Kirby, *"Leadership in the Age of Transparency," Harvard Business Review,* April 2010.

14. The B-Corp movement has been gaining traction over the past several years as a natural outgrowth of efforts by Businesses for Social Responsibility (www.bsr.org) starting in the 1990's. Learn more about it at: www.bcorp.net

15. See Katie Johnston article, "Want more from your workers? Get them to run into each other more often," in *Boston Globe,* Jan 25, 2018.

16. Robert *Putnam's Bowling Alone* (2000), Philip Slater's classic, *The Pursuit of Loneliness* (1970) and Frieda Fromm-Reichmann's article, *Loneliness* (1959) are cornerstones of this work.

17. Much deserved attention has been paid to impacts of social media on political discourse. But this also divides us within our organizations, preventing constructive conversations from occurring across work shifts, classes of employees, and those with divergent views regarding organizational priorities.

18. I've been privileged to work with Darin Harris and Steve Davis since 2007, creating a unique Integral Facilitation model based upon this theory. Through our courses, "Journey of Facilitation and Collaboration" and "Journey Beyond," we apply this approach to developing facilitative leadership capacities that are applicable to a wide range of organizational and community contexts. More information is available at www.journeyofcollaboration.com. In turn, we are indebted to Don Beck, who spent extensive time with Darin, myself, and many colleagues in Madison to teach us about Spiral Dynamics Integral, and to the members of the Madison Integrals Learning Community for their dedication to applying this theory to their workplaces and lives.

19. The Wellness Council of America (WELCOA) has recently published new definitions to guide this conversation. Please check them out and download free resources at www.welcoa.org

20. The Ben and Jerry's model made it a priority to never exceed a 5:1 ratio in compensation between the top managers and entry line staff. It was accompanied by a set of "Compassionate Capitalism Principles" that continue to guide the company, even today, long after the business was sold to Unilever. New CEO Matthew McCarthy seeks to carry on this tradition. Rich DeVos has written about this approach in *Compassionate Capitalism* (1997).

21. Rosen has a related article, *Organization of the Future*, that may be freely downloaded at www.healthycompanies.com, as well as his most recent book, *Conscious: The Power of Awareness in Business and Life* (2018), that updates his thinking and connects well to our discussions here!

22. Thanks to the Office of Human Resources Wellness Committee at University of Wisconsin–Madison for this idea!

23. I first learned about GROW from a chapter by Diane Cory and Rebecca Bradley on "Partnership Coaching," within the book, *Organizational Learning at Work* by John Sterman et al (1998). However, Sir John Whitmore is the likely originator of the GROW Model.

24. This quote has been attributed to Buffett numerous times... I do not know its origin.

25. Buckingham and Clifton, *Now, Discover Your Strengths* (2001) and Rath, *StrengthsFinder 2.0* (2007) are the best introductory resources to the StrengthsFinder assessment tool. Additional work can be done with work teams using Buckingham, *Go Put Your Strengths to Work* (2007) and other resources from Gallup (www.gallup.com) and Buckingham (www.marcusbuckingham.com). I have found it to be very useful in coaching and in helping groups understand their relative strengths and gaps.

26. Diagram taken from Simply Psychology site, article by Saul McClod, updated 2017. Kolb's approach (first published in 1984)

follows a long line of experiential educators, including John Dewey and Jean Piaget, and Maria Montessori. There are many scholarly research articles regarding the efficacy of Kolb's approach, especially in medical education, online learning, and other professional skills development. Kolb's approach is a cornerstone of adult education, and has become integral to much of my work as an educator.

27. For more resources from Russ Harris, see his website: www.actmindfully.au

28. The economist Jacques Attali's "brave and controversial" look at the 21st century (*A Brief History of the Future*, 2006) makes the argument that the economy required to support a new wave of democracy is already forming. He further argues that a reframed view of the Other is at the heart of a new economy that transcends scarcity in service to a greater collective good. It's an important read, especially the final chapter. Then connect his ideas with those of Laloux and his 'next stage' companies (Lesson 12).

29. The investment in resources to facilitate multicultural and multilingual conversations has been well integrated into Canadian engagement processes (though there are definitely areas requiring improvement), but it remains largely an outlier in American approaches to business. A notable success story is the Cultural Linguistic Services office at the University of Wisconsin-Madison: CLS facilitates large-scale deliberations, interprets at interviews and performance reviews, and otherwise is an integral partner in the inclusion and diversity efforts of a large workforce. They have deservedly won kudos for their efforts. See www.talent.wisc.edu and search for "Cultural Linguistic Services." A recent NY Times article illustrates these varied areas of connection, as well as the practical challenges of persevering in the face of marginalization. Alan Henry, *"Productivity Without Privilege: How to Succeed When You're Marginalized or Discriminated Against in the Workplace,"* NY Times, Oct 2, 2019

30. Hersey and Blanchard created the Situational Leadership Model, as a useful way to conceptualize varying leadership roles

and relationships over time and maturity. It has been applied to teams, as well as its initial intention as a resource for managers. See their book, *Management of Organizational Behavior* (1977) or this summary: www.leadership-central.com/situational-leadership-theory.html

31. I took this quote from a presentation that Meg Wheatley gave at the University of Wisconsin–Madison, when I was fortunate enough to host her as part of the first Big Learning Event. The essence of her writing and teaching is that everything comes down to Relationships, and that we need one another to survive and thrive if we are to address the complex leadership challenges of our world. I am grateful for her work and her support.

32. Russ Harris, *ACT Made Simple* (2009), p. 160

33. Finally, I get to acknowledge my partner, Lisa Webne-Behrman, in these notes! She and I developed this approach through our business, Collaborative Initiative, in the early 1990's and have applied it to dozens of workplace, community, and organizational facilitations.

34. This method was developed by the Institute of Cultural Affairs, articulated in Brian Stanfield et al, *The Art of Focused Conversation* (2000). It is an extremely versatile method, applicable to a wide variety of business, community, and public policy situations.

35. There are many excellent resources for those wishing to learn more about addressing conflicts through interest-based, collaborative negotiation. A great starting point is Fisher and Ury, *Getting To Yes* (1983, 2011), followed by other books by the same authors with other collaborators. The work of Bernie Mayer is important, including *The Dynamics of Conflict* (2000) and more recently, *The Conflict Paradox* (2015). Michelle LeBaron is an amazing teacher, mediator, and author of important books in intercultural conflict resolution, including *Bridging Cultural Conflicts* (2009) and *Conflict Across Cultures* (with Vashni Pillay, 2006). The work of Marshall Rosenberg on *Nonviolent Communication* (3rd Edition, 2015), Larry Dressler's *Standing in the Fire* (2010), and Thomas Crum's *The Magic of Conflict* (1998)

are extremely accessible and valuable, with Dressler offering insights that are specifically applicable to group conflict. Finally, I hold in high regard the work of John Paul Lederach, *The Moral Imagination* (2005) and Susan Heitler *From Conflict to Resolution (*1994); while they aren't about conflict in workplace settings, they offer important strategies that can be applied there.

36. Something we haven't discussed here is how groups evolve over time. In my previous book, *The Practice of Facilitation* (1998), I discuss strategies for facilitating groups in various stages of development. But the entire question is often over-simplified - a good resource that maps much closer to my experiences with groups is Scott Peck, *The Different Drum* (2nd Edition, 2010), especially Chapter V on "Stages of Community-Making."

37. Warren Bennis has offered many valuable contributions. One especially relevant to What Matters is *Organizing Genius: The Secrets of Creative Collaboration* (1998).

38. W. Brian Arthur, *The Nature of Technology: What It Is And How It Evolves* (2011). Brian Arthur is an economist who has made immense contributions to our understanding of complexity science. His efforts at the Santa Fe Institute and elsewhere are excellent illustrations of the types of approaches being advocated here.

39. This was described quite well several years ago by Malcolm Gladwell in a New Yorker article, *"In the Air"* (May 12, 2008 issue).

40. Acknowledgment and gratitude to Don Schutt for his support of this idea, which resulted in two great conferences and the birth of an innovative learning community. *"Inspiration from Unusual Sources"* invited people to share their stories of taking creative ideas and transforming them into value-added innovations. The result was a diverse array of experiences, from the sciences and engineering to the arts, and the establishment of true 'out of the box' thinking that inspired further innovations in professional development and staff programs.

41. One fun and useful approach that emerged from UW–MANIAC is called, "Jammin," which is a fast-paced, idea-networking

process. Primarily the result of a collaboration among Darin Eich, Amy Climer, and myself, Jammin' sessions were adapted to facilitate idea-sharing at interdisciplinary scientific gatherings, trainings for new faculty, staff conferences, and other settings. As with so many important innovations, Jammin' began as an idea in Darin's head that led to a quick, small-group cafe conversation, which then was prototyped with a group within two weeks, and evolved into a standard program practice.

42. The UW–MANIAC Tool Box can be accessed at: www.wisc.edu and search for "UW–MANIAC Toolbox".

43. One widespread application of the work of Osborn and Parnes is "Future Problem Solving (FPS)," where participants are provided futuristic scenarios as the basis for teasing out likely issues and creative solutions. School-age children across the world have been taught FPS, and I was fortunate to serve as an FPS evaluator for several years and have adapted it to adults in the workplace.

44. Affinity Diagram Process is a good method to use here, as it promotes collaboration and transparently engages all participants in determining the categories of groups to be used. An excellent resource on this approach is the Interaction Design Foundation: www.interaction-design.org/

45. The set of idea-generating strategies is adapted from the course I co-created with Darin Harris and Steve Davis (see note 18). An important innovator in the process of generating creative ideas is Darin Eich. His book, *Innovation Step-by-Step* (2014) offers a practical overview of his approach. It has been a pleasure collaborating with Darin on various projects over the years; he has much to offer those seeking a greater depth of knowledge in this area. His website is: www.innovationlearning.org

46. An excellent business leadership discussion of this topic comes from David Snowden and Mary Boone, "A Leader's Framework for Decision Making," in *Harvard Business Review*, November 2007.

47. There is far more that can be said regarding what has been learned from complexity science over the past twenty years, including its impacts on business and organizational theory.

An excellent resource (in addition to the work by Adam Kahani cited previously) is Arthur Battram, *Navigating Complexity: The Essential Guide to Complexity Theory in Business and Management* (2001). In addition, the work of Brian Arthur and others at the Santa Fe Institute demonstrates the relationship of complexity to economics; see "Complexity and the Economy," Science, 1999 for a basic overview. Finally, a wonderful consultant offering workshops in this area is Christine Kelly. See her article, "Standing in the Crossroads: The Role of Transformative Education in Addressing Sustainability," *Journal of Sustainability Education*, May 2010.

48. There are several fine teachers and writers in the Appreciative Inquiry field. I recommend Jane Magruder Watkins and Bernard Mohr, *Appreciative Inquiry: Change at the Speed of Imagination* (2001) and David Cooperrider and Diana Whitney, *Appreciative Inquiry: A Positive Revolution in Change* (2005) as good places to start.

49. There are some excellent resources to support World Cafe and other public engagement processes. These include the World Cafe website (www.theworldcafe.com), National Coalition for Dialogue and Deliberation, *Resource Guide on Public Engagement* (2010) and website (www.ncdd.org), and International Association for Public Participation (IAP2), www.iap2.org

50. University Associates (headed by J. William Pfeiffer) produced a series of *"Developing Human Resources"* annuals for many years. They included hundreds of excellent group exercises for a variety of facilitation purposes, often widely tested and researched - their efforts offer a valuable legacy to our field.

51. Once again, I must acknowledge the important contribution of my partner, Lisa Webne-Behrman, in the development and continuous refinement of this process. We have taught it to hundreds of people and it is easily adapted to a wide range of contexts and workplaces where a more informal mediation approach makes sense.

52. Kotter's work is widely used, and it should be an important aspect of our thinking about leading change efforts. Best resources are *Leading Change* (1996, 2012) and *Our Ice is Melting*

(2006). Other excellent resources that have influenced my work include Olson and Eoyang, *Facilitating Organizational Change* (2001) and Rebecca Chan Allen, *Guiding Change Journeys* (2001).

53. A related issue is how to rebuild trust once it has been lost. An excellent resource is the work of Michelle and Dennis Reina. Through their Reina Trust Building Institute, they offer many useful articles, learning aids, and consultancy: www.reinatrustbuilding.com

54. A valid critique of such processes is that they often occur in relative isolation of one another, rather than working in a coordinated manner to leverage the best resources and capacities of each organization engaged in the process. From this concern came some excellent work on "collective impact" from FSG in the US and Tamarack Institute in Canada. See HanleyBrown, Kania, and Kramer, "Channeling Change: Making Collective Impact Work," in *Stanford Social Innovation Review* (2011) and Kabaj and Weaver, "Collective Impact 3.0" (2016) and visit their websites: www.fsg.com and www.tamarackcommunity.ca.

55. Etienne Wenger and colleagues offer several important books and numerous articles, including *Communities of Practice* (2000) and *Cultivating Communities of Practice* (2002), and *Learning in Landscapes of Practice* (2014), among other contributions. His participation as a resource to the development of CoP's at the University of Wisconsin-Madison is greatly appreciated.

56. There is a trove of additional information about these efforts to be found at HR-CoP Office site: www.hr.wisc.edu then look up "HR CoP Office"

57. I want to especially acknowledge Sarah Carroll, who has persevered as an important champion of this Office and the CoP approach with creativity and a powerful commitment to its values, and Leanne Morris, who has really thought carefully about What Matters and integrated it into her career path.

58. Some of the writings that have been most influential for me include Stephen Covey, *The 7 Habits of Highly Effective People* (1998, and more recent editions); Peter Senge, *The Fifth*

Discipline Fieldbook (1994); Margaret Wheatley, *Leadership and the New Science* (1992, 2006) and numerous subsequent books and articles; C Otto Scharmer et al, *Theory U* (2009) and *Presence* (2008); Warren Bennis, *On Becoming a Leader* (1994, 2009) and *Organizing Genius: The Secrets of Creative Collaboration* (2007) and other books on leadership; Robert Greenleaf, *The Power of Servant Leadership* (1998), and other writings with Larry Spears; Joseph Jaworski, *Synchronicity: The Inner Path of Leadership* (2011, 2nd Edition).

59. The "room of requirement" always contains what you need: You simply need to know how to access it! This concept from J. K. Rowling and the *Harry Potter* series offers another example of the "container" offering the resources required if we know how to find them.

60. We have used such a seminar at the University of Wisconsin–Madison since 2007, with excellent, sustained results. Thanks to Kent Lesandrini, Julie Kovalaske, Anne Murphy-Lom (who convened the "Level 5 CoP" that emerged), and the dozens of participants in the Level 4 Leadership Seminar for their energy and wisdom.

61. Excerpt from a poem by Stanley Kunitz, "The Layers," from *The Collected Poems of Stanley Kunitz* (1978), with thanks to Lisa for bringing it to my attention.

62. The idea that we have multiple layers of Identity is important to bring into conversations about all aspects of our lives, including workplace diversity and inclusion (Lesson 18). In the Leadership Institute at the University of Wisconsin–Madison over the past twenty years, convenor Seema Kapani and her colleagues use ongoing, intensive learning communities to explore such questions as a pathway to leadership development ("from everywhere," as we discussed in Lesson 20). I was fortunate to be one of the facilitators in this program for several years, and applaud their continued efforts. See www.lcice.wisc.edu

63. The field of systems thinking owes a major debt of gratitude to Donnella Meadows, whose book, *Thinking in Systems* (2008) was published several years after her death in 2001. It's essential

reading. The use of "biomimicry" in systems design holds much promise in architecture, organizational development, economics, and other areas. Resources include Van Der Ryn and Cowan, *Ecological Design* (1996) and Benyus, *Biomimicry: Innovation Inspired by Nature* (2002). My colleagues Marian Farrior and Erin Schneider offer excellent workshops in this area, and we utilize such examples in fostering transformative change in the "Journey of Facilitation and Collaboration" and "Journey Beyond" course I co-teach with Steve Davis and Darin Harris (www.journeyofcollaboration.com).

WORKS CITED

Arthur, W. Brian. *The Nature of Technology: What It Is and How It Evolves.* Free Press, 2011.

Bell, Daniel. *The Coming of Post-Industrial Society: a Venture in Social Forecasting.* Basic Books, 1973.

Bennis, Warren, *On Becoming a Leader*, Basic Books, 1994, 2009.

Bennis, Warren and Patricia Ward Biederman, *Organizing Genius: The Secrets of Creative Collaboration*, Basic Books, 1997.

Benyus, Jeanine, *Biomimicry: Innovation Inspired by Nature*, William Morrow, 2002.

Bergonzi, Bernard. *T. S. Eliot: Four Quartets: a Selection of Critical Essays.* Macmillan, 1987.

Block, Peter. *Community: the Structure of Belonging.* BK, Berrett-Koehler Publishers Inc. a BK Business Book., 2018.

Bridges, William, and Susan Bridges. *Managing Transitions: Making the Most of Change.* Nicholas Brealey Publishing, 2017.

Brown, Juanita, and David Isaacs. *The World Café: Shaping Our Futures through Conversations That Matter.* Berrett-Koehler Publishers Inc., 2006.

Buckingham, Marcus, and Donald O. Clifton. *Now, Discover Your Strengths: How to Develop Your Talents and Those of the People You Manage.* Pocket Books, 2005.

Collins, Jim. Good to Great: *Why Some Companies Make the Leap ... and Others Don't.* HarperTrade, 2001.

Collins, Rod. *Wiki Management: a Revolutionary New Model for a Rapidly Changing and Collaborative World.* American Management Association, 2014.

Cooperrider, David L. *Appreciative Inquiry: an Emerging Direction for Organization Development.* Stipes, 2001.

Cooperrider, David and Diana Whitney, *Appreciative Inquiry: A Positive Revolution in Change*, Barrett-Koehler, 2005.

Covey, Stephen, *The Seven Habits of Highly Effective People*, 1998, 2013 (25th Anniversary Edition).

Eich, Darin, *Innovation Step By Step*, Amazon Books, 2014.

Fisher, Roger, and William Ury. *Getting to Yes: Negotiating an Agreement without Giving In.* Random House Business, 2012.

Greenleaf, Robert K., and Larry C. Spears. *The Power of Servant-Leadership: Essays.* RHYW, 2014.

Greenleaf, Robert K. *The Servant as Leader.* Center for Applied Studies, 1973.

HBR's 10 Must Reads 2017: the Definitive Management Ideas of the Year from Harvard Business Review. Harvard Business Review Press, 2017.

Harris, Russ. *ACT Made Simple: an Easy-to-Read Primer on Acceptance and Commitment Therapy.* New Harbinger Publications, Inc., 2009.

Hersey, Paul and Ken Blanchard, *Management of Organizational Behavior*, Prentice-Hall, 1977.

Heitler, Susan M, *From Conflict to Resolution: Skills and Strategies for Individual, Couple, and Family Therapy*, Norton, 1993.

Hesselbein, Frances, et al. *The Organization of the Future.* Jossey-Bass Publishers, 1997.

Holman, Peggy, et al. *The Change Handbook: the Definitive Resource on Today's Best Methods for Engaging Whole Systems.* Berrett-Koehler, 2007.

Jaworski, Joseph, *Synchronicity: The Inner Path of Leadership*, 1998, 2011, Amazon Books.

Kahani, Adam, *Transformative Scenario Planning*, Berrett-Koehler Books, 2012.

Kaner, Sam, *Facilitator's Guide to Participatory Decision-Making*, Jossey-Bass, 2014.

Kelley, David and Thomas, *Creative Confidence*, Crown Business, 2013.

Laloux, Frederic. *Reinventing Organizations a Guide to Creating Organizations Inspired by the next Stage of Human Consciousness.* Nelson Parker, 2014.

Laloux, Frederic, *Reinventing Organizations a Guide to Creating Organizations Inspired by the next Stage of Human Consciousness.* Nelson Parker, 2014.

LeBaron, Michelle, *Bridging Cultural Conflicts*, John Wiley, 2004.

LeBaron, Michelle and Venashri Pillay, *Conflict Across Cultures*, 2016.

Lederach, John Paul, *The Moral Imagination*, Oxford University Press, 2010.

Lightman, Alan P., and Grover Gardner, *Einstein's Dreams*. 2015.

Lipmanowicz, Henri, and Keith McCandless. *The Surprising Power of Liberating Structures: Simple Rules to Unleash a Culture of Innovation*. Liberating Structures Press, 2016.

Mayer, Bernard, *The Dynamics of Conflict*, 2nd Edition, John Wiley & Sons, 2012.

Mayer, Bernard, *The Conflict Paradox*, Jossey-Bass, 2015.

McGregor, Douglas, and Joel Cutcher-Gershenfeld, *The Human Side of Enterprise*, 1960; McGraw-Hill 2006.

McKeown, J. *Essentialism: The Disciplined Pursuit of Less*. Virgin Books, 2014.

Meadows, Donnella, *Thinking in Systems: A Primer*, Chelsea Green Publishing, 2008.

Naisbitt, John. *Megatrends: Ten New Directions Transforming Our Lives.* Publisher Not Identified, 1985.

Osland, Joyce, et al. *Organizational Behavior: an Experiential Approach.* Prentice Hall, 2001.

Patterson, Kerry, et al. *Crucial Conversations.* McGraw-Hill, 2012.

Patton, Michael Quinn. *Developmental Evaluation: Applying Complexity Concepts to Enhance Innovation and Us*e. Guilford Press, 2011.

Patton, Michael Quinn. *Utilization-Focused Evaluation.* SAGE Publications, Inc, 2008.

Peck, M. Scott, *The Different Drum: Community-Making and Peace,* 1987.

Rosen, Robert H., and Lisa Berger. *The Healthy Company: Eight Strategies to Develop People, Productivity and Profits.* Tarcher, 1992.

Ryan, Kathleen D., and Daniel K. Oestreich. *Driving Fear out of the Workplace: Creating the High-Trust, High-Performance Organization.* Jossey-Bass, 1998.

Scharmer, C. Otto, *Theory U: Leading from the Future as it Happens,* Berrett-Koehler, 2006.

Scharmer, C. Otto et al, *Presence: An Exploration of Profound Change in People, Organizations, and Society,* Crown Business, 2005.

Schein, Edgar H. *Humble Consulting: How to Provide Real Help Faster.* Read How You Want, 2016.

Schein, Edgar H. *Humble Inquiry: The Gentle Art of Asking Instead of Telling.* Berrett-Koehler Publishers, Inc., 2014.

Senge, Peter et al, *The Fifth Discipline Fieldbook: Practices and Strategies for Building a Learning Organization*, Crown Business, 1994.

Sinek, Simon. *Start with Why: How Great Leaders Inspire Everyone to Take Action*. Penguin Business, 2019.

Slater, Philip, *The Pursuit of Loneliness*, Beacon Press, 1970.

Smith, Rolf. *The 7 Levels of Change: Diffferent Thinking for Diffferent Results*. Tapestry Press, 2011.

Stanfield, R. Brian. *The Art of Focused Conversation: 100 Ways to Access Group Wisdom in the Workplace*. New Society Publishers, 2013.

Stone, Douglas, et al. *Difficult Conversations: How to Discuss What Matters Most*. Penguin Books, 2010.

Magruder Watkins, Jane, Ralph Kelly and Bernard Mohr, *Appreciative Inquiry: Change at the Speed of Imagination*, Pfeiffer, 2001.

Van Der Ryn and Cowan, *Ecological Design*, Island Press 1996, 2007.

Webne-Behrman, Harry, *The Practice of Facilitation: Managing Group Process and Solving Problems*, Quorum Books, 1998.

Webne-Behrman, Harry, *Guardian of the Process*, Collaborative Initiative, Inc., 1994.

Wenger, Etienne, and William Snyder. *Communities of Practice: the Organizational Frontier*. Harvard Business Review, Jan-Feb 2000.

Wenger, Etienne, et al. *Cultivating Communities of Practice: a Guide to Managing Knowledge*. Harvard Business School Press, 2010.

Wenger, Etienne, et al. *Digital Habitats: Stewarding Technology for Communities*. CPsquare, 2009.

Wenger, Etienne. *Learning in Landscapes of Practice: Boundaries, Identity, and Knowledgeability in Practice-Based Learning.* Langara College, 2017.

Wheatley, Margaret J. *Finding Our Way: Leadership for an Uncertain Time.* Berrett-Koehler, 2005.

Wheatley, Margaret J. *Leadership and the New Science: Learning About Organization from An Orderly Universe.* First Edition, 1992.

Whyte, David. *Crossing the Unknown Sea: Work and the Shaping of Identity.* Penguin, 2002.

Whyte, David. *The Three Marriages: Reimagining Work, Self and Relationship.* Riverhead Books, 2010.

Zander, Rosamund Stone, and Benjamin Zander. *The Art of Possibility: Practices in Leadership, Relationship, and Passion.* Michael Joseph, 2006.

APPENDIX A: SCENARIOS

Collaborative Approaches to Conflict Management

The following scenarios represent common workplace conflicts. Identify situations that you believe are worth practicing. Form small groups, practice these situations as they align with our goals, and take this opportunity to improve your skills in this important area.

The Angry Customer

An angry customer has come into your office, berating you and your staff for the way a problem has been addressed. This person is demanding a change in the problem determination, and is quite aggressive and loud about the matter.

The Outside Relationship

Two co-workers are involved in a significant personal relationship outside of the office. At work, they are neglecting their duties and "stealing away" to spend time together. Others on the staff are upset, both morally and practically, and have complained to you as the supervisor to do something about it.

Outside Interests

One of your staff members routinely talks about outside interests and recreational activities at work, often coming into people's work areas and interrupting their work with stories. People have complained to you about it, but this person has been at your agency for a long time and you are reluctant to make a big deal out of it.

Overwhelmed

A person you supervise is overwhelmed by the workload, resulting in projects you manage being delayed. While you are sympathetic, and you realize that this staff member receives work from others as well, you are frustrated by an apparent lack of organization or taking responsibility. Excuses are made whenever confronted.

The Argument

Two co-workers are involved in a heated argument at work. You notice what is happening, but not being their supervisor, you are reluctant to become involved. Still, you feel strongly that they need to calm down and behave professionally.

Defending the Policy

Executive Committee has directed you to implement a policy that you believe will have negative impacts on your department's ability to deliver services. Your manager has told you to "be a good soldier" and support the policy in your discussions with your staff. However, you believe in maintaining an honest working relationship with your staff, and feel such an attitude would compromise that relationship. You want to get your manager to understand this, and to support you on a different approach with your staff. You also believe your manager could have done more to prevent this policy change from occurring.

Following Procedures

A staff member recently informed you of plans to take a vacation next week, during a very busy work time in your office. They felt this was a routine confirmation of notice that had been given three months ago, but you only vaguely recall such a conversation and never received a "Vacation Request Form." Given the workload, you are upset at being put in this position, and you know that others will resent it. But this is a valued employee who plays a key role on your staff.

Avoided Performance Issues

You are a new Manager of your department. You have a staff member who has been with the department for many years, and several staff have warned you that this person malingers, misses work time as much as possible, and fully utilizes the cover of "the union" to avoid work. As part of your effort to meet individually with all staff members, you now realize that you need to set clear expectations regarding work performance for everyone, as communication has been inconsistent. In your short tenure as Manager, you realize the concerns about this staff member may be valid, based upon what you have observed. However, there is nothing in the personnel file to indicate less than satisfactory performance over the years; i.e., the problems seem to have been largely avoided.

Mediation Skills for Managers

Terms are useful here: The "Initiator" is the person who has requested mediation, while the "Respondent" is the person who has responded to the request. The "Mediator" is someone who plays an impartial, facilitative role, supporting the two conflicting people in their efforts to communicate, understand one another, and reach mutually acceptable agreements regarding their concerns.

The Overwhelmed Co-Worker

Initiator: Sal

A co-worker, Pat, is overwhelmed by the workload, resulting in projects you manage being delayed. While you are sympathetic, and you realize that he receives work from others, as well, you are frustrated by an apparent lack of organization or taking responsibility. Pat makes excuses whenever confronted. You are not Pat's supervisor; the supervisor doesn't seem to be engaged in dealing with the poor work performance, either. Overall, you are pretty upset!

Respondent: Pat

Your workload has been horrific, especially since those two positions were lost last year. At this point, you are worried about your job security. And you can tell that your relationships with co-workers are getting strained, especially people like Sal who depend upon you for their own projects. But, without additional help, it's really beyond your control! Sal knows we lost those positions, and should be more supportive of your situation!

The Veteran and the Newbie

Initiator: Max

I am Max. I have been at the Department for only a few months, and while I'm only in my late 20's, I have had a great deal of success elsewhere with innovative programs. I was hired to be creative and help us move into new areas, but I'm feeling stifled at every turn from Sam.

Sam has been with the Department for many years, and has accomplished a great deal in that time. But the reputation is now clearly outdated, as Sam hasn't produced anything, it seems, for years and spends most of the time out of the office (at the tavern?). At a recent staff meeting, I brought up some new ideas about how to improve services to respond to current student needs, but Sam just put me down (in front of everyone); Sam constantly disrespects my experience!

Respondent: Sam

I am Sam, and I've been a Program Manager in the Department for over 20 years. I've seen it all around here, and over time I have managed to earn a pretty decent reputation and set of working relationships with colleagues across campus. I'm looking forward to retirement in a few years, but hope to leave the Department in good shape, with my programs and services (hopefully) surviving the budget cuts.

Max is new to the Agency, and brings some youthful energy to the place. I was optimistic when Max was hired, but now I am concerned that there is some immaturity and impatience that cannot be overcome. Perhaps Max is self-absorbed and doesn't realize the impact of their communication style on others? If you are going to be successful here, you have to 'pay your dues' and patiently work through the bureaucracy.

Deadlines

Initiator: Laura

I am Lead for the IT Team of the Sirius Project, a major grant-funded initiative that began last year. I have been at Superior Group for several years, and joined this project a few months ago. One member of my IT Team is Jose, an experienced staff member with some great database management skills. But Jose never follows through on his commitments to the team, and doesn't seem to even care about our deadlines! Every time I ask him about when we can expect his work, he is pretty vague, saying something like, "It'll come together when it's ready, Laura..." I've had it! [Note: We can also add cultural or gender bias into this scenario.]

Respondent: Jose

I am a member of the IT Team of the Sirius Project, a major grant-funded initiative that began last year. I have been at Superior Group for several years, mostly working on database development and management. This is a very interesting project, with lots of opportunities for innovation. But it is also a highly complex project, so people need to be patient about letting us write all of the programs and test them adequately so we aren't forced to go back later. In addition, Laura (the Team Lead) keeps coming to me with unrealistic demands about deadlines, AND at the same time the Director (of the Project) comes to me with new ideas about what the database should be able to do. I'm overwhelmed and confused! I try to tell her, "It'll come together when it's ready, Laura...", but she is so high-strung! [Note: We can also add an element of cultural or gender bias to this scenario]

More to Life than Work

Initiator: D

I don't understand why G is so hurtful! I just want to live my life and go about doing my job, without interference. But I find that hard to do with all of the gossip, back-biting, and polarizing that G promotes. G is constantly talking about what others are doing, speculating about who is 'in' or 'out' with the boss, and distracting us from our work. It wasn't so bad my first few months here, but it has gotten very hurtful, and just plain filled with false information. G doesn't like me, because I don't get into it, and then turns others against me. Who has time for this nonsense? I never experienced anything like this in my previous department!

Respondent: G

D needs to understand that there has to be more to life than work, which can be tedious and boring in this administrative office. Maybe it works in some departments, where you live a leisurely life without tight deadlines, but these jobs are stressful and you need a release. D just doesn't cooperate and isn't friendly: D never goes to lunch with us, seems really private, and sulks around – I wonder if there are problems at home? We get our work done, so there isn't any reason to complain... if we end up with more work as a result of this mediation stuff, I'll be ticked!

R-E-S-P-E-C-T

Initiator: Mal (Department Head)

Lee is simply not cooperating with the rest of the staff. While I've tolerated this personality over the years, I'm tired of this insensitive, self-centered approach! There is no coordination or collaboration on projects, office hours are not honored (so people can never find Lee), and the only things Lee seems to invest energy in are pet projects and outside interests. Lee waltzes into the Dept. Office with piles of work, forms, etc. that require immediate attention and disrupts the staff, acting indignant when they don't immediately respond... and I get to hear it! As a long-tenured staff member with a big reputation, there is little I can practically do - but I need to try! Or else...

[Be sure to place in a context for further details...]

Respondent: Lee

I've been here 15 years and deserve greater respect than I am being given at this point by Mal. As Department Head, Mal should respect the independence of the experienced, veteran staff and work on things that really require attention: budgets, space, mentoring new employees, keeping upper Management off our backs, etc. I produce results, continue to publish widely in the field, and participate extensively in professional conferences. I realize that takes me away from the office sometimes, but it shouldn't be of any concern to anyone else; I'm not alone in this regard and shouldn't be singled out. So what if I miss some office hours... my customers can access me, and they are the ones that really matter here...

[Be sure to place in a context for further details...]

Sharing the Load

"Sharing the Load" is a meeting initiated by the Director, who is facilitating the discussion between J and C, two staff members who are both Project Team Leaders. C has been with the department for 7 years, while J has been here for 3 years. C is more conservative and traditional in the job approach, with many years of prior experience, while J is recently out of school, and has lots of energy and spends extra hours at work...

Team Lead: J

There is so much work to do around this place, and C never seems to be around to pick up anything that needs help! What is it that C does all week? The rest of us have our jobs, but we also 'pick up' for one another and support each other. And this department is expected to generate revenue, too – if not, jobs might get cut (mine, since I'm lower in seniority)! I'm really upset with the Director for letting C get away with this stuff... I certainly don't want to get into trouble or seem non-cooperative in this meeting, but I'm reluctant to share how I truly feel.

Team Lead: C

I've been in this field for over 20 years and pride myself in working pretty efficiently at this point. I also have outside interests, such as my family and my involvement in community theatre, which takes many evenings. As such, I appreciate that I can come to work, do my job, leave and not be 'burned out.' J is clearly in a different place in life, without family or other responsibilities and trying to 'get ahead' around here. J does a good job... pretty inefficient at this point, but quality work that we value here as the Department grows. We need new programs and revenue sources, so J's energy will be key. I'm not really sure why we are meeting with Director, except that we need to assess how best to share the workload for the year ahead... I'm not sure why the three of us are meeting, since it ought to involve the other staff members, as well...

Creative Problem Solving

Moving the Operation

The Service Center has operated successfully on the east side of the city for many years. It is a highly regarded operation with many loyal customers and long-term staff. The SC has outgrown its space, so it is moving across town to a brand new facility. While customers and staff were surveyed regarding potential services at the new location, they were never asked about the qualities of the new space or the impact of the new location on their abilities to get to work or receive services. Staff were consulted by the architects to determine office needs and priorities, but senior staff and managers were given preference for private offices, rather than looking at which job functions required confidentiality. To save money, only a few offices have windows... most of the light entering the building is in public, customer-facing spaces.

Re-Org at Robertson and Company

After many years, Robertson and Company is making a significant shift in its operations. Traditionally it was a clear hierarchy, with discrete departments and reporting lines. But today's employees seek more autonomy, and they often need to work in cross-functional project teams. So Robertson and Company is implementing a new structure that places greater emphasis on fluid project teams that draw upon the best workers for the job. Team leaders will be assigned on the basis of skills and experience for that project, and reporting lines will be determined by governance groups that take on such responsibilities. While there will be a six month transition period, it is expected that the new organization will be fully in place after that time.

APPENDIX B: WORKSHEETS

Desired Calendar

Step 1

At the start of the day, create your own "Desired Calendar" for the day. Using whatever technology suits you (paper, online calendar, phone, etc.), list and review the tasks you wish to accomplish today.

If you were to create an "agenda" of these items, identify specific objectives associated with each one - for today only - and the time likely needed.

If connecting with others is required, be sure to consider when in the sequence of task completion that is likely to occur.

Insert "project time" into your day, using your calendar to block it out.

Step 2

Repeat this process each day for a week. Adjust in order to realistically fit your priorities and Intentions.

Desired Calendar (cont.)

Intentions: Date:

Tasks	
Reflections	
Next Steps	

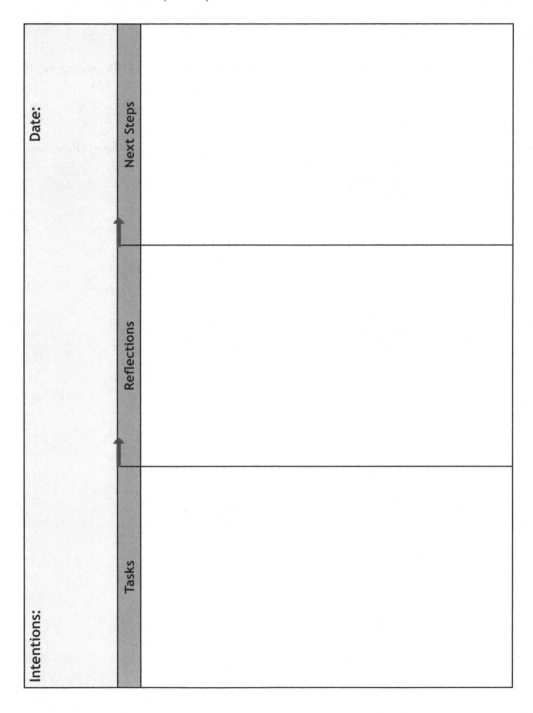

Coat of Arms

Step 1

In each box, represent a value that matters to you in your life and work. It may be a picture, phrase, or other artistic representation.

Step 2

At the bottom, insert a simple Motto that captures the essence of the values that guide you.

Coat of Arms (cont.)

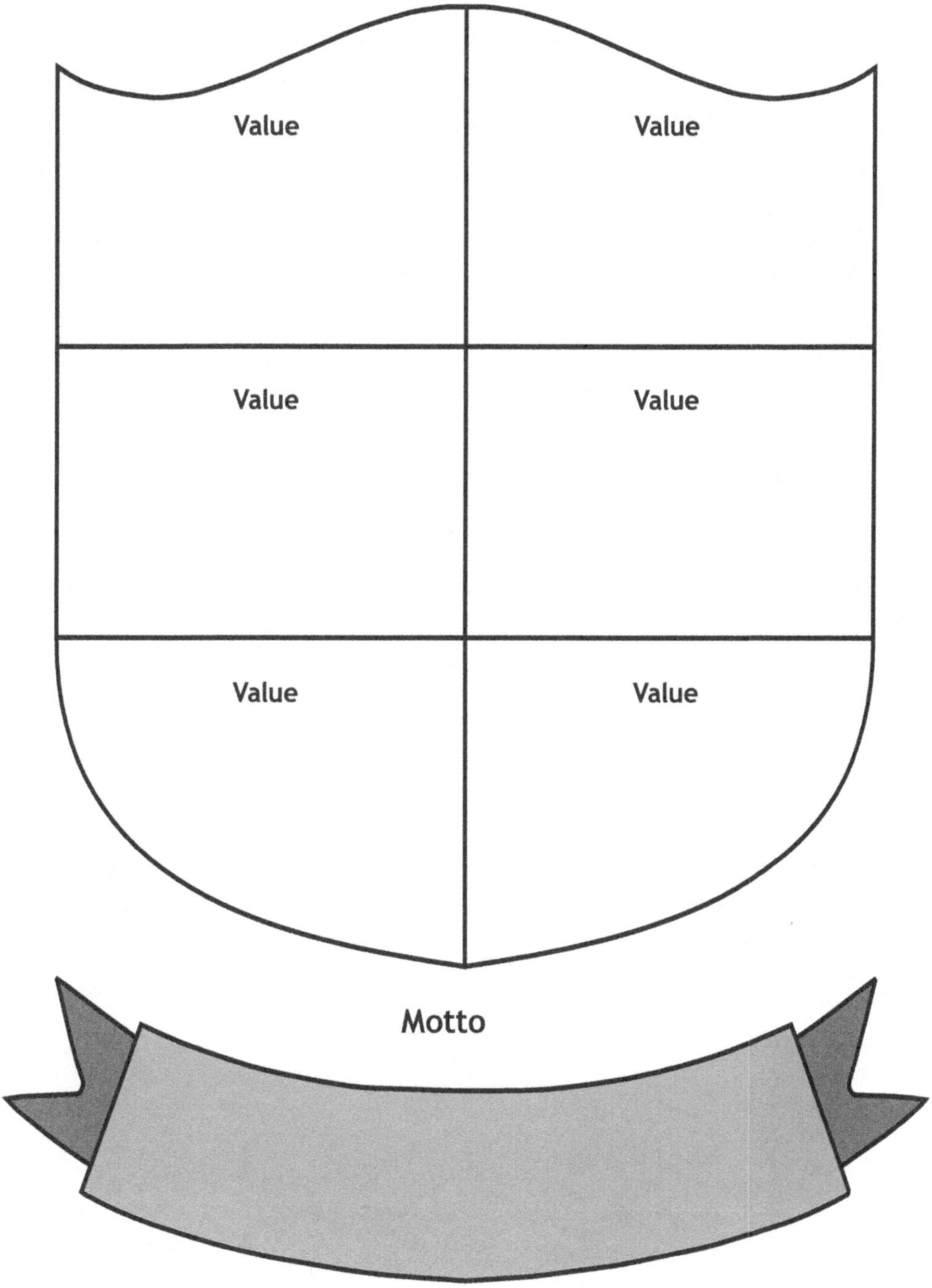

Values, Behaviors, and Desired Change

Step 1

Write your Core Values across the top of the sheet. Then notice Smith's "7 Levels" headings down the left side.

Step 2

Using the cells created by points of intersection, enter Actions that can be taken that align values and levels of change.

Step 3

Consider:

- What's emerging for you?
- Where do you notice repeated Actions that seem to Matter at this time to you and your organization?

Step 4

Discuss the results with a colleague (alternatively, this can be a group exercise).

- What are some Desired Outcomes that appear as a result of this initial thinking?

Step 5

Save these results - we will engage in later activities that can build upon this work. Smith's book is also a great resource here, offering activities at each level.

Values, Behaviors, and Desired Change (cont.)

	Core Value:	Core Value:	Core Value:
LEVEL 1: Do the right thing			
LEVEL 2: Do the thing right			
LEVEL 3: Do things better			
LEVEL 4: Do away with things			
LEVEL 5: Do what others are doing			
LEVEL 6: Do what no one else is doing			
LEVEL 7: Do what can't be done			

Information and Communication Flow

Consider communication and information sharing in your organization.

A. How timely is relevant information shared?

B. How complete and meaningful is the communication?

C. Who "owns" the decision to share information? How does that influence others' sense that they can and should share information?

D. How transparent is the sharing of information internally? Externally?

Information and Communication Flow (cont.)

E. What are the natural consequences of these levels of transparency for relationships, problem-solving, decision-making, and learning?

F. What constraints exist that prevent more complete and transparent communication? To what degree are you able to influence or modify any of these constraints?

G. In what ways is there intentional balance between autonomy of staff to determine what is needed, and the role of group/team information sharing?

Goal-Reality-Options-Will (GROW)

Questions for Peer Coaching

GOALS (specific, measurable, realistic)

What do you want?

- What would you like to achieve or accomplish?
- If you could create anything you want, what might that be?
- What would ultimate success look like to you?
- How will you know when you have achieved your goal?

REALITY (starting point)

What is happening now?

- How do you feel about what is happening now?
- What is the bigger "lay of the land"? How do you feel about it?
- What have others expressed about the situation? What have you tried thus far?
- What other involved persons might you talk to for additional reflection?

OPTIONS

What might you do?

- What are all the different things you might do? What else might you do?
- If money/time/resources were no obstacle, what options might you choose?
- If you were to ask person X, what might he or she suggest?
- What resources or tools do you have at your disposal?
- Would you like to hear some ideas that have occurred to me?

WILL (actionable, accountable)

What will you do?

- Where would you like to begin? Where do you have energy?
- Which options would you like to explore further?

Actionable

- What are all the different things you might do? What else might you do?

Accountable

- What steps are involved?
- How will you track your progress/revisit these goals?
- How will you hold yourself accountable?

GROW (cont.)

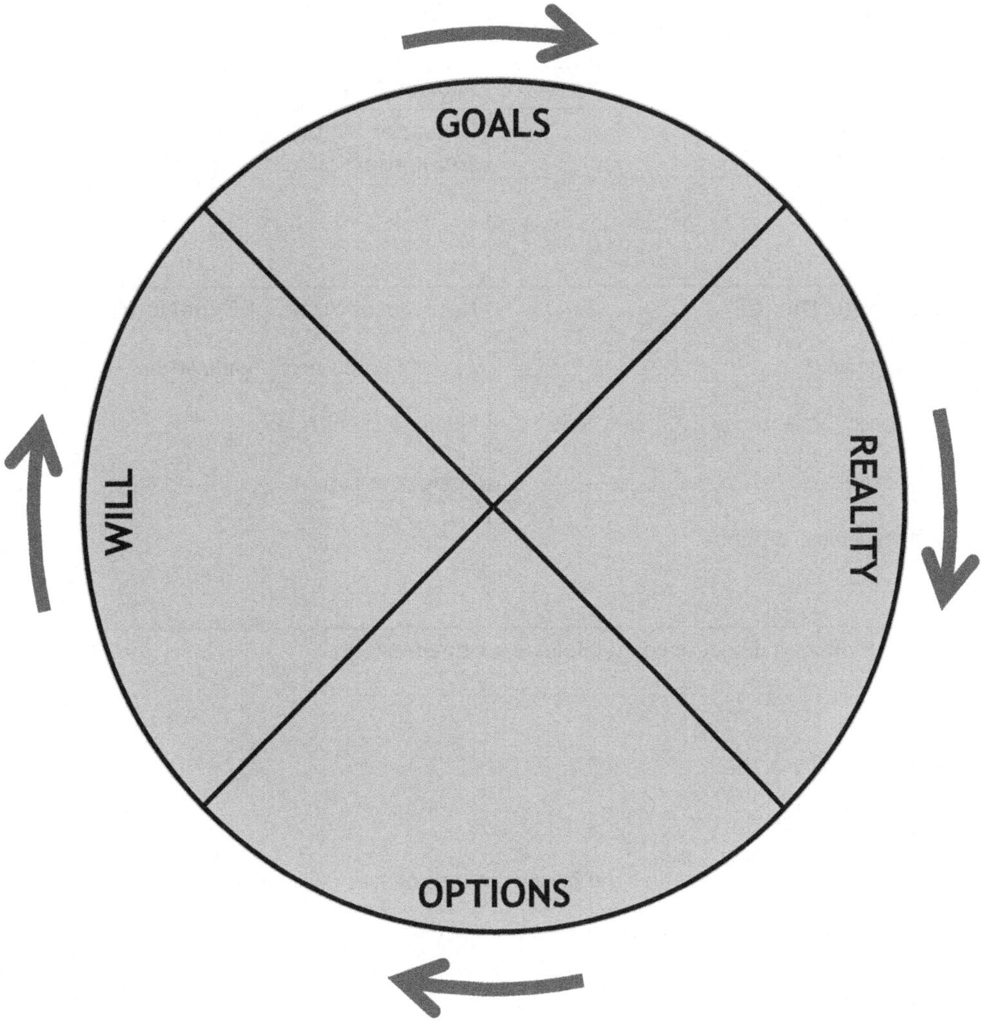

Gathered/inspired from *Partnership Coaching* by Diane Cory and Rebecca Bradley, and *The GROW Model*.

Individual Development Plan

Name:	
Current Position:	**Payroll Title:**
Today's Date:	**Dates for follow-up meetings with supervisor:** (at least once every three months)
Purpose for the IDP ☐ New to Role ☐ Increase Competency in Current Role ☐ Change Role ☐ Other, please describe:	**Number of Years of Experience** At this (or another) organization: In your current role: Doing your current type of work:

Career Plan (You do not need a plan for each timeframe.)

Immediate:

Short-term (1-2 years):

Long-term (3-5 years):

How will your career plans meet the business needs of your division or unit?

If you are interested in a new role, list 2-3 potential next positions:

Professional Development Goals - Professional development involves gaining new skills, knowledge, and/or competencies. What kind of professional development do you need in order be successful with your career plan? List one or two SMART goals (Specific, Measurable, Achievable, Realistic, Timely)

Professional Development Goal 1:

Professional Development Goal 2:

Individual Development Plan (cont.)

Professional Developmental Goal:					Date:
Skills, knowledge, or competencies to be developed:					
Development Activity Classes, E-learning, Education, Readings Learning from Others Learning by Doing On-the-Job	**Description of Activity**	**Outcomes/ Results** What will success look like?	**Support/ Resources Needed** Who will support you? What resources do you need?	**Target Dates** When will the activity be completed? What are the major milestones?	**Status** How are you progressing? What are potential road blocks? What strategies can you use?

Difficult Conversation

Step 1

Reflect on these questions before having the conversation:

- How do you define this conversation? What are your frames for the substantive, emotional, and identity conversations contained within it?
- What specific changes do you seek as a result of this conversation? Is it clear why these changes matter to you?
- What would you like the other person to understand as a result of this conversation?
- How will you know the changes that result will have addressed your needs in the substantive, emotional, and identity conversations?

Step 2

Answer the above questions, then find a partner or colleague with whom to practice this conversation. Help your partner understand the likely answers to these questions from the perspective of the real person you are imagining here. Follow the ORID levels of inquiry to keep the conversation focused. As appropriate, after practicing, have a genuine meaningful conversation with the other person(s) involved in the situation.

Step 3

After practicing (or after a real conversation) reflect:

- How well did the conversation align with my expectations?
- To what degree were desired results achieved?
- What supported or undermined our ability to achieve the desired results?
- How did my behavior contribute to the success of the conversation?
- How did it inhibit such efforts?

Sorting Our Challenges

Step 1

Describe an important challenge your organization (or you) are facing at this time:

Step 2

What types of problems are contained within this challenge? (Label and place in one of the categories: Simple, Complicated, Complex, and Chaotic, as a way to map your current understanding of the situation.

Step 3

Then consider:

- Are we treating these issues appropriately?
- Are the right people involved in trying to address them?
- Are the people addressing these issues provided appropriate resource and training to address them successfully?
- Are we communicating appropriate expectations regarding each issue, given its nature?

Sorting Our Challenges (cont.)

Problem	Simple	Complicated	Complex	Chaotic

About the Author

Harry Webne-Behrman has served as a facilitator, consultant, educator, and mediator for over 40 years. Along with his wife, Lisa Webne-Behrman, he served as Senior Partner of Collaborative Initiative, Inc., a private consulting and mediation firm based in Madison, Wisconsin from 1991-2017. Harry has worked with hundreds of businesses, educational institutions, community groups and public agencies, helping address entrenched organizational and social issues. By consulting with leaders, facilitating large-scale deliberation and engagement processes, mediating interpersonal disputes, and offering educational programs that develop skills needed to address such challenges, Harry has earned a reputation as a valued resource and guide. He maintains tremendous enthusiasm about the importance of learning to work collaboratively to build positive work environments, and offers ***What Matters at Work*** courses and consultations in that spirit.

Harry has also worked with the University of Wisconsin–Madison in numerous capacities. Most recently, he served as Founding Director of the HR Communities of Practice Office. In that capacity, he led development of an array of new learning communities and competency-based certification pathways that support professional development of Human Resources staff across the University. Harry continues to offer professional and executive leadership development courses for UW–Madison through the Center for Professional and Executive Development in the Wisconsin School of Business, as well as the Office of Learning and Talent Development.

In 2006, Harry received the Wisconsin Association of Mediators Distinguished Service Award in recognition of his extensive contributions to the field, and received a UW–Madison Employee Recognition Award in 2013. In addition to ***What Matters At Work***, Harry is the author of ***The Practice of Facilitation*** (1998), ***Guardian of the Process*** (1994), and co-author of the ***Working It Out Series*** (1991-96) in peer mediation and conflict resolution education in schools, and has authored numerous articles on mediation, conflict resolution, and facilitation. Harry and Lisa now live and work in Ottawa, Ontario.

More about What Matters at Work:
Contact Harry at **harry.whatmatters@gmail.com**
Visit the blog: **www.whatmattersatwork.ca**